Heinz-Gerhard Justenhoven, James Turner (Eds.)

Rethinking the State in the Age of Globalisation

POLITIK
Forschung und Wissenschaft

Band 10

LIT

Heinz-Gerhard Justenhoven, James Turner (Eds.)

Rethinking the State in the Age of Globalisation

Catholic Thought
and Contemporary Political Theory

LIT

Cover Picture: Ernst Helmstädter

Satz und Lektorat: Gabi Trillhaas, Rodgau
lektorat@trillhaas.com

Bibliographic information published by Die Deutsche Bibliothek
Die Deutsche Bibliothek lists this publication in the Deutsche
Nationalbibliografie; detailed bibliographic data are available in the
Internet at http://dnb.ddb.de.

ISBN 3-8258-7249-1

© LIT VERLAG Münster   2003
Grevener Str./Fresnostr. 2   48159 Münster
Tel. 0251-23 50 91   Fax 0251-23 19 72
e-Mail: lit@lit-verlag.de   http://www.lit-verlag.de

Distributed in North America by:

Transaction Publishers
New Brunswick (U.S.A.) and London (U.K.)

Transaction Publishers   Tel.: (732) 445 - 2280
Rutgers University   Fax: (732) 445 - 3138
35 Berrue Circle   for orders (U. S. only):
Piscataway, NJ 08854   toll free (888) 999 - 6778

Contents

Introduction   7

Stephen D. Krasner
    Four Meanings of Sovereignty   15

Penny Gill
    Mastering Globalization:
    State-Building and Sovereignty in the EU   45

James Bernard Murphy
    Aristotelian Political Science:
    Bildungspolitik and the End of Sovereignty   73

Kenneth Pennington
    Sovereignty and Rights in Medieval and
    Early Modern Jurisprudence:
    Law and Norms without a State   117

Norbert Brieskorn SJ
    Universalism and Particularism according to
    Francisco Suárez   143

Heinz-Gerhard Justenhoven
    Peace through a Public Global Authority in
    Papal Teaching from Leo XIII to John XXIII   167

Klaus Dicke
　Sovereignty under Law　195

Matthias Lutz-Bachmann
　The Sovereignty Principle and Global Democracy:
　Thoughts on Transforming the System of States,
　Based on Kant　217

Authors　233

Introduction

Since Jean Bodin and Thomas Hobbes, political theorists have depicted the state as "sovereign" because it holds preeminent authority over all the denizens belonging to its geographically defined territory. This idea of sovereignty invested the state with both independence from any higher earthly authority or judge and the right to wage war without moral or juridical limitation. Moreover, since the nineteenth century, sovereignty has been associated with the assumption that the people claiming the territory constitute a single "nation". From the Peace of Westphalia in 1648 until the beginning of World War I in 1914, the essential responsibilities ascribed to the sovereign state were maintaining internal and external security and promoting domestic prosperity.

This idea of "the state" in political theory is clearly inadequate to the realities of national governments and international relations at the beginning of the twenty-first century. It simply fails to explain how real governments function today. During the twentieth century, the sovereign state, as a reality and an idea, has been variously challenged from without and within its borders. World War I brought mass destruction in Europe that exposed the limits of sovereignty. The League of Nations aimed to curtail the state's unrestrained right to wage war. More ambitiously, the United Nations, by moving toward making the use of violence a collective prerogative, has reconfigured international security questions. Meanwhile, international courts have treated a widening list of human rights as integral to international law and expanded the scope of international justice. Since the end of World War II, terrorism, organized crime, and environmental dangers have emerged as international risks. The aggregation of enterprises in every sector into transnational corporations is still accelerating. Individual nations often seek to respond to these challenges by cooperating in conferences and organizations on the international level and ceding limited parts of their sovereignty.

However, in the first chapter in this book this widely accepted thesis of the decline of state sovereignty in the twentieth century is called into question by *Stephen Krasner*. He distinguishes four aspects of sovereignty. All four can apply to a single state, but they need not: States are regarded as sovereign without fulfilling all four requirements. Finally, Krasner states, some aspects of sovereignty have at all times been absent or violated. He therefore denies the standard thesis that erosion of sovereignty is a new development, resulting from globalization.

In any case, the sovereign state, while remaining the primary actor in international politics, is at least changing its role and even its self-definition. In this situation the current discussion of globalization is trying to catch up with events. How can we adequately describe the process? Is the reality of sovereignty changing, or is the idea of sovereignty being replaced by something different? *Penny Gill* offers her view of the process of globalization and its effects on societies, states and sovereignty. Gill points to the European controversy about the result of transferring sovereignty to the EU. Does this shift of sovereignty weaken national states or – on the contrary – actually strengthen the political legitimacy of individual states by increasing their overall political effectiveness on the global level? The European Union, which Gill understands as a European effort to master the challenges of globalization, is considered a laboratory to test what sovereignty means in the post-modern world. In accord with the principle of subsidiarity, sovereignty seems to be becoming diversi-fied and fragmented, ascending to the European level on one hand (fiscal policy) and descending to the sub-national level on the other (cultural policy). This is a process similar to the one that the United States underwent in forming the union at the end of the eighteenth century. Summing up what is transferred to the EU level, Gill sees the EU as fullfilling key tasks of a modern state but showing a lack of democracy in doing so.

Must we – can we? – develop new conceptions of the state more adequate to the challenges of domestic and international politics and governance in today's world? Are Catholic intellectual traditions of any help in devising effective criteria for what many see as the post-state era? Is it possible to derive from Catholic intellectual traditions criteria to which political units and institutions will conform? Within Catholic thinking about society, there is a focus on the human being as the purpose and end of every political entity, whether local, regional, national or universal. In consequence, the state is never an end in itself, as extreme nationalist positions suppose, but a means of preserving the dignity of persons.

Catholic political thinking owes much to the merger of the Artistotelian tradition with medieval theology, a marriage seen at its best in Thomas Aquinas. *James B. Murphy* investigates the moral principles of Aristotelian political science, focusing on the relation of ethical deliberation and the political dimension. To reconstruct Aristotle's political science, he compares it to Thomas Aquinas' ideas. According to Murphy, Aristotelian political ethics does not focus on individual well-being and the conditions of society required to foster it. On the contrary the highest aim of politics according to Aristotle is to encourage the individual to aspire to the good. In consequence politics should be setting the conditions that meet those needs best.

Catholic political theory has throughout its history been sceptical of the idea of sovereignty. Historically it tended to oppose assertions of absolute sovereignty and favor instead a universalistic ideal, the "orbis christianus." *Kenneth Pennington* gives some insight into the rationale of that position, explicating the relation of the rights of the individual to the sovereignty of the emerging state of the late medieval period. His material basis is the *ius commune*, Europe's universal law from the twelfth to the seventeenth century. The jurists of that period had a common understanding of law in the sense of sharing a set of norms focusing on the protection of the rights of the individual, in a way that modern constitutions never did. This common, Europe-wide understanding limited the sovereignty of the emerging state in this but also in other regards. The rise of absolutism and "national" laws led to the decline of the traditional Europe-wide law. Now the prospect of European integration challenges political theorists to consider again this ancient juridical concept of limited sovereignty.

In the age of discovery the medieval universalistic idea came up against challenges that would have been incomprehensible earlier. The most elaborated response revolved around the question, did the Indian population in the newly discovered American world have genuine "human rights"? Innumerable Spanish theologians and jurists of the sixteenth and seventeenth century got involved in this intellectual and political dispute. *Norbert Brieskorn* shows how the great scholastic thinker Francisco Suárez reflected on the intellectual background of his age and developed from it his own theory: A theory of how to relate Old and New Worlds, the individual state and the universal community of states. In explaining his notions of natural law, law of nations, common good, and universal society, Brieskorn brings together Suárez's views on universality, the universal society, and particularism, the particular state.

At the end of the nineteenth century the focus of theology and of papal texts in particular shifted to the "social question." Beginning with Leo XIII, the popes displayed growing concern over the arms build-up among the European powers and later over the massive destruction of the First and then the Second World War. *Heinz-Gerhard Justenhoven* shows how the popes, beginning with Benedict XV, strove to develop a political framework founded on natural law: On the basis of an international law, operating through effective international institutions, war should be overcome. The sovereign state would not only lose its right to wage war but would become subject to international law. In papal teaching the state is seen as functioning to serve the individual. Deploying the category of the common good, the popes aimed to confine the state to its necessary tasks while advocating a supranational authority to meet the needs of the international community.

But can states maintain their sovereignty under international law? *Klaus Dicke* would clearly say yes. He depicts a version of sovereignty adapted to the changes wrought by globalization. Following Kant, he defines sovereignty as an "expression of autonomy by political entities" against threats to their freedom from within and without their community. Looking to international law and mainly to the United Nations charter, Dicke describes the change during the twentieth century from the exclusive authority of nation states above any law to their sovereign equality under international law. The perceptions of sovereignty by different states are too various to draw from them any understanding of what sovereignty today really means. According to Dicke, an adequate notion of sovereignty in today's world has rather to be developed from the goal of statehood - the well-being of its people - in a globalized world, where global problems are dealt with by states together with non-state actors.

The shift of the sovereignty of nation states into other hands - whether this be to internal actors at the substate level or external actors at the suprastate level - raises the question of whether these new agents on the political scene are democratically legitimate. *Matthias Lutz-Bachmann* decries what he sees as a deficit of democratic legitimization in this change in the structure of political action. Transporting Kant's political philosophy into the globalized political world of the twenty-first century, he concludes the necessity of a "globally applicable world law" proceeding from the "united will of the world's citizens" and a consensus on essential human rights. How could the preservation of those essential human rights be universally and impartially guaranteed? Lutz-Bachmann advocates some sort of universal statehood, though with the imperative of the principle of subsidiarity ensuring the political self-determination of the individual.

These challenging chapters derive from a conference convened in Berlin in September 2000 by *Institut für Theologie und*

Frieden and *Erasmus Institute*. The conferees were asked to explore specific ways in which the intellectual traditions of Catholicism might help our effort to rethink the state. We organized the conference in the conviction that those intellectual resources would prove valuable to political theorists as they work to revise our understanding of the state. We hope the valuable discussion begun in Berlin and extended in these pages will continue beyond them.

Heinz-Gerhard Justenhoven James Turner

Four Meanings of Sovereignty[1]

Stephen D. Krasner

The term sovereignty has been commonly used in at least four different ways: domestic sovereignty, referring to the organization of public authority within a state and to the level of effective control exercised by those holding authority; interdependence sovereignty, referring to the ability of public authorities to control transborder movements; international legal sovereignty, referring to the mutual recognition of states or other entities; and Westphalian sovereignty, referring to the exclusion of external actors from domestic authority configurations. These four meanings of sovereignty are not logically coupled, nor have they covaried in practice.

Embedded in these four usages of the term is a fundamental distinction between authority and control. Authority involves a mutually recognized right for an actor to engage in specific kinds of activities. If authority is effective, force or compulsion would never have to be exercised. Authority would be coterminous with control. But control can be achieved simply through the use of brute force with no mutual recognition of authority at all. In practice, the boundary between control and authority can be hazy. A loss of control over a period of time could lead to a loss of authority. The effective exercise of control, or the acceptance of a rule for purely instrumental reasons, could

---

1. First published in: Stephen D. Krasner, *Sovereignty. Organized Hypocrisy*. Princeton, NJ, 1999, 9-25.

generate new systems of authority. If a practice works, individuals might come to regard it as normatively binding, not just instrumentally efficacious; conversely, if a mutually accepted rule fails to control behavior, its authority might be rejected over time.[2] In many social and political situations both a logic of consequences, in which control is the key issue, and a logic of appropriateness, associated with authority, can both affect the behavior of actors.[3]

Westphalian sovereignty and international legal sovereignty exclusively refer to issues of authority: does the state have the right to exclude external actors, and is a state recognized as having the authority to engage in international agreements? Interdependence sovereignty exclusively refers to control: can a state control movements across its own borders? Domestic sovereignty is used in ways that refer to both authority and control: what authority structures are recognized within a state, and how effective is their level of control? A loss of interdependence sovereignty (control over transborder flows) would almost certainly imply a loss of domestic sovereignty in the sense of domestic control but would not necessarily imply that the state had lost domestic authority.[4]

---

2. Sugden (1989) in his discussion of evolutionary game theory suggests that a rule that is initially accepted for purely consequential reasons can come to be normatively binding, authoritative, over time, because it works and is generally accepted.

3. For further discussions of the distinction between authority and control with reference to sovereignty, see Wendt and Friedheim 1996, 246, 251; Onuf 1991, 430; Wendt 1992, 412-13; Shue, 1997, 348.

4. Similar distinctions are developed by Thomson (1995) who emphasizes the critical difference between control on the one hand, which may be threatened by what is called here a loss of interdependence sovereignty, and authority on the other. Daniel Deudney has also noted the different ways in

Domestic Sovereignty

The intellectual history of the term sovereignty is most closely associated with domestic sovereignty. How is public authority organized within the state? How effectively is it exercised? Bodin and Hobbes, the two most important early theorists of sovereignty, were both driven by a desire to provide an intellectual rationale for the legitimacy of some one final source of authority within the state. Both were anxious to weaken support for the religious wars that tore France and Britain apart by demonstrating that revolt against the sovereign could never be legitimate.[5] Strayer, in his study of the early state, suggests that "For those who were skeptical about the divine right of monarchs there was the theory that the state was absolutely necessary for human welfare, and that the concentration of power which we call sovereignty was essential for the existence of the state."[6] F. H. Hinsley

---

which the term sovereignty has been used and confounded. Deudney defines sovereignty as the ultimate source of authority in the polity. "This meaning of sovereignty," he goes on to point out, "is often conflated with the related questions of authority, which refers to the exercise of legitimate power (what is here termed an aspect of domestic sovereignty), autonomy, which refers to the independence of a polity vis-a-vis other polities (which is here referred to as Westphalian sovereignty), and recognized autonomy, which involves the rights, roles, and responsibilities of membership in a society of states (which is called in this study international legal sovereignty)" (1995,198). Although Cerny does not explicitly use the term sovereignty, he also makes a set of distinctions that recognize the difference between internal and external autonomy. Internally states can be strong or weak. Externally they can be dependent or autonomous. A state that is internally weak and externally dependent is classified by Cerny (1990,101) as penetrated.

5. Skinner 1978, 287
6. Strayer 1970, 108.

writes, "at the beginning, at any rate, the idea of sovereignty was the idea that there is a final and absolute political authority in the political community; and everything that needs to be added to complete the definition is added if this statement is continued in the following words: 'and no final and absolute authority exists elsewhere'".[7] Later theorists from Locke, to Mill, to Marx, to Dahl have challenged the notion that there has to be some one final source of authority, but the work of all of these writers is concerned primarily with the organization of authority within the state.

Polities can be organized in many different ways without raising any issues for either international legal or Westphalian sovereignty. Authority may be concentrated in the hands of one individual, as Bodin and Hobbes advocated, or divided among different institutions, as is the case in the United States. There can be federal or unitary structures. The one point at which the organization of domestic authority could affect international legal sovereignty occurs in the case of confederations in which the individual units of the state have some ability to conduct external relations.[8]

The effectiveness of political authorities within their own borders may also vary without empirically or logically influencing international legal or Westphalian sovereignty. Whether operating in a parliamentary or presidential, monarchical or republican, or authoritarian or democratic polity, political leaders might, or might not, be able to control developments within their

---

7. Hinsley 1986, 25-26.

8. This was the case, for instance, for Bavaria, which retained the right to independent foreign representation, although largely for honorary purposes, after German unification in 1870. Oppenheim 1992, 247; Brierly 1963, 127-28.

own territory. They might, or might not, be able to maintain order, collect taxes, regulate pornography, repress drug use, prevent abortion, minimize corruption, or control crime. A state with very limited effective domestic control could still have complete international legal sovereignty. It could still be recognized as a juridical equal by other states, and its representatives could still exercise their full voting rights in international organizations. The Westphalian sovereignty of an ineffective state would not necessarily be compromised. Domestic leaders might continue to exclude external actors, especially if these actors were not much interested in local developments. Domestic sovereignty, the organization and effectiveness of political authority, is the single most important question for political analysis, but the organization of authority within a state and the level of control enjoyed by the state are not necessarily related to international legal or Westphalian sovereignty.

Interdependence Sovereignty

In contemporary discourse it has become commonplace for observers to note that state sovereignty is being eroded by globalization. Such analysts are concerned fundamentally with questions of control, not authority.[9] The inability to regulate the flow of goods, persons, pollutants, diseases, and ideas across territorial boundaries has been described as a loss of sovereignty.[10] In his classic study, *The Economics of Interdependence,* Richard Cooper argued that in a world of large open capital mar-

---

9. Thomson 1995, 216
10. Mathews 1997; Wriston 1997.

kets smaller states would not be able to control their own monetary policy because they could not control the transborder movements of capital. James Rosenau suggests in *Turbulence in World Politics* that the basic nature of the international system is changing. The scope of activities over which states can effectively exercise control is declining. New issues have emerged such as "atmospheric pollution, terrorism, the drug trade, currency crises, and AIDS," which are a product of interdependence or new technologies and which are transnational rather than national. States cannot provide solutions to these and other issues.[11]

While a loss of interdependence sovereignty does not necessarily imply anything about domestic sovereignty understood as the organization of authoritative decision making, it does undermine domestic sovereignty comprehended simply as control. If a state cannot regulate what passes across its borders, it will not be able to control what happens within them.

It is nowhere near as self-evident as many observers have suggested that the international environment at the end of the twentieth century has reached unprecedented levels of openness that are placing new and unique strains on states. By some measures international capital markets were more open before the First World War than they are now.[12] The importance of international trade has followed a similar trajectory, growing during the last half of the nineteenth century, then falling from the first to the fifth decades of the twentieth century, then growing after 1950 to unprecedented levels for most but not all states.[13] International

---

11. Rosenau 1990, 13.

12. Obstfeld and Taylor 1997.

13. Thomson and Krasner 1989.

labor movements were more open in the nineteenth century than they are now.[14] Some areas have become more deeply enmeshed in the international environment, especially East Asia; others, notably most of Africa, remain much more isolated. Regardless of the conclusions that are reached about changes in international flows, there have still been considerable variations in national political responses. Increases in transnational flows have not made states impotent with regard to pursuing national policy agendas; increasing transnational flows have not necessarily undermined state control. Indeed, the level of government spending for developed countries has increased along with various measures of globalization since 1950.[15]

Interdependence sovereignty, or the lack thereof, is not practically or logically related to international legal or Westphalian sovereignty. A state can be recognized as a juridical equal by other states and still be unable to control movements across its own borders. Unregulated transborder movements do not imply that a state is subject to external structures of authority, which would be a violation of Westphalian sovereignty. Rulers can lose control of transborder flows and still be recognized and be able to exclude external actors.

In practice, however, a loss of interdependence sovereignty might lead rulers to compromise their Westphalian sovereignty. Indeed, neoliberal institutionalism suggests that technological changes, which have reduced the costs of transportation and communication, have led to a loss of interdependence sovereignty, which, in turn, has prompted states to enter into agreements (an exercise of international legal sovereignty) to create international institutions, some of which have compro-

---

14. Williamson 1996, 16, 18, table 2.1.

15. Garrett 1998.

mised their Westphalian sovereignty by establishing external authority structures.[16]

Thus the first two meanings of sovereignty, interdependence sovereignty and domestic sovereignty, are logically distinct from the basic concerns of this study — international legal sovereignty and Westphalian sovereignty. The structure of domestic political authority and the extent of control over activities within and across territorial boundaries are not necessarily related to international recognition or the exclusion of external actors, although behaviorally the erosion of domestic or interdependence sovereignty can lead rulers to compromise their Westphalian sovereignty.

International Legal Sovereignty

The third meaning of sovereignty, international legal sovereignty, has been concerned with establishing the status of a political entity in the international system. Is a state recognized by other states? Is it accepted as a juridical equal? Are its representatives entitled to diplomatic immunity? Can it be a member of international organizations? Can its representatives enter into agreements with other entities? This is the concept used most frequently in international legal scholarship, but it has been employed by scholars and practitioners of international relations more generally.

The classic model of international law is a replication of the liberal theory of the state. The state is treated at the international level as analogous to the individual at the national level.

---

16. Keohane 1984, 1995,

Sovereignty, independence, and consent are comparable with the position that the individual has in the liberal theory of the state.[17] States are equal in the same way that individuals are equal. The concept of the equality of states was introduced into international law by Vattel in *Le droit de gens,* first published 1758. Vattel reasoned from the logic of the state of nature. If men were equal in the state of nature, then states were also free and equal and living in a state of nature. For Vattel a small republic was no less a sovereign state than was a powerful kingdom.[18]

The basic rule for international legal sovereignty is that recognition is extended to entities, states, with territory and formal juridical autonomy. This has been the common, although as we shall see, not exclusive, practice. There have also been additional criteria applied to the recognition of specific governments rather than states: the Communist government in China, for instance, as opposed to the state of China. These additional rules, which have varied over time, have included the ability to defend and protect a defined territory, the existence of an established government, and the presence of a population.[19]

The supplementary rules for recognizing specific governments, as opposed to states, have never been consistently applied. The decision to recognize or withhold recognition can be a political act that can support or weaken a target government. Weaker states have sometimes argued that the recognition of governments should be automatic, but stronger states, who might choose to use recognition as a political instrument, have rejected this principle. States have recognized other governments even when they did not

---

17. Weiler 1991, 2479-80.

18. Brierly 1963, 37-40.

19. Fowler and Bunck 1995, chap. 2; Thomson 1995, 228; Oppenheim 1992, 186-90; Crawford 1996, 500.

have effective control over their claimed territory, such as the German and Italian recognition of the Franco regime in 1936, and the American recognition of the Lon Nol government in Cambodia in 1970. States have continued to recognize governments that have lost power, including Mexican recognition of the Spanish republican regime until 1977, and recognition of the Chinese Nationalist regime by all of the major Western powers until the 1970s. States have refused to recognize new governments even when they have established effective control, such as the British refusal in the nineteenth century to recognize the newly independent Latin American states until a decade after they had established effective control, the Russian refusal to recognize the July monarchy in France until 1832, and the U.S. refusal to recognize the Soviet regime until 1934. The frequency and effectiveness of the use of recognition or nonrecognition as a political instrument have depended both upon the distribution of power (conflicting policies by major powers reduce the impact of recognition policies) and the degree of ideological conflict.[20]

More interesting is not the fact that specific governments have been denied or given recognition, but rather that even entities, as opposed to specific governments, that do not conform with the basic norm of appropriateness associated with international legal sovereignty have been recognized. Entities that lack either formal juridical autonomy or territory have also been recognized. India was a member of the League of Nations and a signatory of the Versailles settlements even though it was a colony of Britain. The British Dominions were signatories at Versailles and members of the league even though their juridical independence from Britain was unclear. India and the Philippines were founding members of the United Nations even though they did not become

---

20. M. Peterson 1982, 328-36; Peterson 1997, 32, 90-91, 187; Strang 1996, 24.

formally independent until 1946 and 1947 respectively. The Palestinian Liberation Organization (PLO) was given observer status in the United Nations in 1974 and this status was changed to that of a mission in 1988 coincident with the declaration of Palestinian independence even though the PLO did not have any independent control over territory. Byelorussia and the Ukraine were members of the United Nations even though they were part of the Soviet Union.[21] Andorra became a member of the United Nations in 1993 even though France and Spain have control over its security affairs and retain the right to appoint two of the four members of its Constitutional Tribunal.[22] Hong Kong, a British colony and then part of China, became a founding member of the World Trade Organization even though China was not. The Order of Malta is recognized as a sovereign person by more than sixty states even though it lost control of Malta in 1798 and holds no territory other than some buildings in Rome.[23]

The uncertainty surrounding the recognition of specific governments, and even the violations of the principle that recognition should be limited to territorial entities that are juridically independent, have not reduced the attractiveness of international legal sovereignty for rulers or created an environment in which basic institutional arrangements have been challenged.

Almost all rulers have sought international legal sovereignty, the recognition of other states, because it provides them with both material and normative resources. Sovereignty can be conceived of as "a ticket of general admission to the international

---

21. Oppenheim 1992, 145-46.

22. Constitution of Andorra 1993, Article 66.

23. Bradford 1972, 63-67, 117-23, 220, 226.

arena."[24] All recognized states have juridical equality. International law is based on the consent of states. Recognized states can enter into treaties with each other, and these treaties will generally be operative even if the government changes. Dependent or subordinate territories do not generally have the right to conclude international agreements (although, as with everything else in the international system, there are exceptions), giving the central or recognized authority a monopoly over formal arrangements with other states.[25]

Even though the differences in treatment can be blurred, it is better to be recognized than not. Nonrecognition is not a bar to the conduct of commercial and even diplomatic discourse, but it can introduce an element of uncertainty into the calculations of actors. Ex ante they may not be able to predict how particular governments or national court systems will respond to an unrecognized government.[26] Multinational firms might be more reluctant to invest.

By facilitating accords, international legal sovereignty offers the possibility for rulers to secure external resources that can enhance their ability to stay in power and to promote the security, economic, and ideational interests of their constituents. The rulers of internationally recognized states can sit at the table. Entering into certain kinds of contracts, such as alliances, can enhance security by reducing uncertainty about the commitment of other actors.[27] Membership in international financial institutions opens

---

24. Fowler and Bunck 1995, 12.
25. Oppenheim 1992, 158, 245, 339-40; Thomson 1995, 219.
26. For a discussion of the relationship between the Sovereign Immunities Act in the United States and recognition, see Movsesian 1996.
27. Fowler and Bunck 1995, 142.

the possibility, although not the assurance, of securing foreign capital. Even if rulers have entered into accords that have far-reaching effects on their domestic autonomy, such as the European Union, they have nothing to lose by retaining their international legal sovereignty, including their formal right to withdraw from any international agreements.

Recognition also provides a state, and by implication its rulers, with a more secure status in the courts of other states. The act of state doctrine holds, in the words of one U.S. Supreme Court decision, that "Every sovereign State is bound to respect the independence of every other sovereign State, and the courts of one country will not sit in judgment on the acts of the government of another done within its own territory."[28] In British and American courts recognition is consequential because the sovereign or public acts of a recognized state, as opposed to its private or commercial acts, cannot be challenged, and the property of a recognized state is immune from seizure. Traditionally only the citizens of recognized states have been able to appear as parties to litigation in the United States. If a government or state is not recognized either de jure or de facto, then American and British courts need not consider its legislation valid—for instance, in deciding whether a piece of property has been legally transferred.[29]

Recognition also provides immunity for diplomatic representatives from both civil and criminal actions. Representatives are not subject to any form of arrest or detention, although the host country can refuse to receive, or can expel, specific individuals. Diplomatic premises can not be entered by representatives of

---

28. The case is *Underhill vs. Hernandez,* quoted in Oppenheim 1992, 365-67.

29. Brierly 1963, 149-50.

the host country. Diplomatic bags can not be opened.[30]

The attractiveness of international legal sovereignty can also be understood from a more sociological or cognitive perspective. Recognition as a state is a widely, almost universally understood construct in the contemporary world. A ruler attempting to strengthen his own position by creating or reinforcing a particular national identity is more likely to be successful if his state or his government enjoys international recognition. Recognition gives the ruler the opportunity to play on the international stage; even if it is only a bit part, parading at the United Nations or shaking hands with the president of the United States or the chancellor of Germany can enhance the standing of a ruler among his or her own followers. In an uncertain domestic political situation (a situation in which domestic sovereignty is problematic), international recognition can reinforce the position of rulers by signaling to constituents that a ruler may have access to international resources, including alliances and sovereign lending. Hence, international legal sovereignty can promote the interests of rulers by making it easier for them to generate domestic political support not just because they are in a better position to promote the interests of their constituents but also because recognition is a signal about the viability of a political regime and its leaders.

Like other institutional arrangements in the international environment, however, international recognition is not a constitutive act in the sense that the absence of recognition precludes the kinds of activities that recognition itself facilitates. Governments have maintained administrative contacts and signed agreements with governments they have not recognized; they have exchanged trade missions, registered trademarks, accepted consular missions, and concluded arrangements for the exchange of prisoners of war.

---

30. Oppenheim 1992, 1072-97.

Representatives of one state have had contacts with representatives of other states that they have not recognized; for instance, the United States sent a personal representative to the Holy See when the Vatican was not recognized by the United States; U.S. and mainland Chinese officials met in Geneva in 1954; the Vietnam peace negotiations in Paris from 1970 to 1973 took place when the United States did not recognize the North Vietnamese government; President Nixon went on an official visit to China in 1971 when the two countries did not recognize each other. National court systems have increasingly been given discretion by their own governments to decide whether the actions of nonrecognized governments will be given special legal standing. The U.S. Protection of Diplomats Act of 1971 provides for the protection of diplomats even if their governments have not been recognized by the United States. When the United States recognized the People's Republic of China as the legitimate government of China in 1979 and withdrew recognition from the Republic of China (ROC), it established a special status for Taiwan. The Taiwan Relations Act stipulated that the legal standing of the ROC in American courts would not be affected, that Taiwan would continue to be a member of international financial institutions, and that the American Institute in Taiwan, a nongovernmental agency, would be created, in effect, to conduct the functions of an embassy.[31] Whatever international recognition has meant, it has not led rulers to eschew efforts to alter the domestic authority structures, policies, or even personnel of other states, or to enter into contractual relationships that compromise the autonomy of their own state. International legal sovereignty does not mean Westphalian sovereignty. Moreover, it does not guarantee that legitimate domestic authorities

---

31. Oppenheim 1992, 158-73; M. Peterson 1997, 107-8, 140, 148-52, 197; United States, Taiwan Relations Act.

will be able to monitor and regulate developments within the territory of their state or flows across their borders; that is, it does not guarantee either domestic sovereignty or interdependence sovereignty.[32]

Indeed, international legal sovereignty is the necessary condition for rulers to compromise voluntarily aspects of their Westphalian sovereignty. Nowhere is this more apparent than in the European Union. In an interview shortly before the opening of the April 1996 European Union conference on governance in Turin, Jacques Chirac, the president of France, stated that "In order for Europe to be widened it must in the first instance be deepened, but the sovereignty of each state must be respected."[33] Chirac was arguing that the member states of the European Union must retain their international legal sovereignty, even while they were entering into agreements that compromised their Westphalian interdependence, and domestic sovereignty since the

---

32. With American troops about to leave Italy in the summer of 1947 following the ratification of the Italian Peace Treaty, George Marshall, the American secretary of state, indicated to the U.S. embassy in Rome that it must be stressed to General Lee (commander of allied forces) that "Govt Allied mil in Italy must respect scrupulously restoration Ital sovereignty upon coming into force treaty" (United States, FRUS, [1947, vol. 3], 1972, 931). This message was sent at time when the United States was intervening in Italian domestic politics by supporting the Christian Democrats, trying to restructure the Socialist Party, and attempting to weaken the position of the Communist Party in Italy. Marshall wanted to recognize Italy's international legal sovereignty, but he was completely unconcerned with Italy's Westphalian sovereignty, with the exclusion of American influence from Italy's domestic authority formations. See Miller 1986, 243-63.

33. *Frankfurter Allgemeine Zeitung*, March 26, 1996, 1, translated by the author. The original quotation reads: "Um sich erweitern zu können, muss sich Europa zunächst vertiefen, wobei es die Souveränität seiner Staaten respektieren muss."

European Union can regulate transborder movements; the European Court exercises transnational authority; and some European Union decisions can be taken by a majority vote of the member states.

Finally, it should be obvious that international legal sovereignty does not guarantee the territorial integrity of any state or even the existence of a state. Recognized states have been dismembered and even absorbed. The conquest of any particular state extinguishes the sovereignty of that state (domestic, Westphalian, interdependence, and usually international legal), but conquest is not a challenge to Westphalian and international legal sovereignty as institutional forms. It reconfigures borders but does not create new principles and norms.

Westphalian Sovereignty

Finally, sovereignty has been understood as the Westphalian model, an institutional arrangement for organizing political life that is based on two principles: territoriality and the exclusion of external actors from domestic authority structures. Rulers may be constrained, sometimes severely, by the external environment, but they are still free to choose the institutions and policies they regard as optimal. Westphalian sovereignty is violated when external actors influence or determine domestic authority structures.

Domestic authority structures can be infiltrated through both coercive and voluntary actions, through intervention and invitation. Foreign actors, usually the rulers of other states, can use their material capabilities to dictate or coerce changes in the authority structures of a target; they can violate the rule of nonintervention in the internal affairs of other states. Rulers may also themselves establish supranational or extranational authority structures that constrain their own domestic autonomy; they can extend invitations, sometimes inadvertent, that result in compromises of their own Westphalian sovereignty. While coercion, intervention, is inconsistent with international legal as well as Westphalian sovereignty, voluntary actions by rulers, invitations, do not violate international legal sovereignty although they do transgress Westphalian sovereignty.

The norm of nonintervention in internal affairs had virtually nothing to do with the Peace of Westphalia, which was signed in 1648. It was not clearly articulated until the end of the eighteenth century. Nevertheless, the common terminology is used here because the Westphalian model has so much entered into common usage, even if it is historically inaccurate.

The fundamental norm of Westphalian sovereignty is that states exist in specific territories, within which domestic political authorities are the sole arbiters of legitimate behavior. While autonomy can be compromised as a result of both intervention and invitation, the former has gotten much more attention. For many observers, the rule of nonintervention - which is always violated through coercion or imposition, as opposed to voluntary invitation - is the key element of sovereign statehood. Robert Jackson writes that: "The *grundnorm* of such a political arrangement (sovereign statehood) is the basic prohibition against foreign intervention which simultaneously imposes a duty of forbearance and confers a right of independence on all statesmen. Since states are profoundly unequal in power the rule is obviously far more constraining for powerful states and far more liberating for weak states."[34]

The principle of nonintervention was first explicitly articulated by Wolff and Vattel during the last half of the

---

34. Jackson 1990, 6.

ticulated by Wolff and Vattel during the last half of the eighteenth century. Wolff wrote in the 1760s that "To interfere in the government of another, in whatever way indeed that may be done, is opposed to the natural liberty of nations, by virtue of which one is altogether independent of the will of other nations in its action."[35] Vattel argued that no state had the right to intervene in the internal affairs of other states. He applied this argument to non-European as well as European states, claiming that "The Spaniards violated all rules when they set themselves up as judges of the Inca Athualpa. If that prince had violated the law of nations with respect to them, they would have had a right to punish him. But they accused him of having put some of his subjects to death, of having had several wives, &c—things, for which he was not at all accountable to them; and, to fill up the measure of their extravagant injustice, they condemned him by the laws of Spain."[36]

Weaker states have always been the strongest supporters of the rule of nonintervention. During the nineteenth century the Latin American states endorsed this rule at international meetings in 1826 and 1848. In 1868 the Argentine jurist Carlos Calvo published a treatise in which he condemned intervention by foreign powers to enforce contractual obligations of private parties. The foreign minister of Argentina, Luis Drago, argued in a note to the American government in 1902 that intervention to enforce the collection of public debts was illegitimate. The Calvo and Drago doctrines became recognized claims in international law. At the sixth International Conference of American States held in Havana in 1928, the Commission of Jurists recommended adoption of the principle that "No state has a right to interfere in the internal affairs of another." This proposal, however, was

---

35. Quoted in A. Thomas and Thomas 1956, 5.
36. Vattel 1852, 155.

rejected, in large part because of the opposition of the United States. The United States had engaged in several interventions in Central America and the Caribbean. The American secretary of state, Charles Evans Hughes, argued that the United States had a right to intervene to protect the lives of its nationals should order break down in another country. At the seventh International Conference of American States held in 1933, the United States finally accepted the principle of nonintervention. The wording that "no state has the right to intervene in the internal or external affairs of another" was included in the Convention on Rights and Duties of States and accepted by the United States.[37] The Charter of the Organization of American States (OAS) stipulates that "No State or group of States has the right to intervene, directly or indirectly, for any reason whatever, in the internal or external affairs of any other State. The foregoing principle prohibits not only armed force but also any other form of interference or attempted threat against the personality of the State or against its political, economic, and cultural elements."[38] In the latter part of the twentieth century nonintervention has been routinely endorsed in major international agreements such as the United Nations Charter and the 1975 Helsinki agreement, albeit often along with other principles such as human rights that are in tension with nonintervention.

While Westphalian sovereignty can be compromised through invitation as well as intervention, invitation has received less notice in the literature because observers have confounded international legal and Westphalian sovereignty. Intervention violates both. Invitation violates only Westphalian sovereignty. Invitation occurs when a ruler voluntarily compromises the

---

37. A. Thomas and Thomas 1956, 56-62.
38. Quoted in Damrosch 1993.

domestic autonomy of his or her own polity. Free choices are never inconsistent with international legal sovereignty.[39]

Invitations can, however, infringe domestic autonomy. Rulers may issue invitations for a variety of reasons, including tying the hands of their successors, securing external financial resources, and strengthening domestic support for values that they, themselves, embrace. Invitations may sometimes be inadvertent; rulers might not realize that entering into an agreement may alter their own domestic institutional arrangements. Regardless of the motivation or the perspicacity of rulers, invitations violate Westphalian sovereignty by subjecting internal authority structures to external constraints. The rulings of the European Court of Justice, for instance, have legitimacy in the judicial systems of the member states of the European Union. IMF conditionality agreements, which may include stipulations requiring changes in domestic structures, carry weight not only because they are attached to the provision of funding but also because the IMF has legitimacy for some actors in borrowing countries derived from its claims to technical expertise. Human rights conventions can provide focal points that alter conceptions of legitimacy among groups in civil society and precipitate possibly unanticipated changes in the institutional arrangements of signatory states.

Violations of Westphalian sovereignty can arise in a sovereign state system because the absence of a formal hierarchical system of authority, the defining characteristic of any international system, does not mean that the authority structures in any

---

39. Oppenheim (1992, 431), for instance, writes that intervention only occurs when one state engages in forcible or dictatorial measures related to matters over which another state has the right to exercise sovereignty, such as "its political, economic, social and cultural systems, and its foreign policy."

given political entity will be free of external influence. Wendt and Friedheim have defined informal empires as "transnational structures of de facto political authority in which members are juridically sovereign states."[40] Formal constitutional independence does not guarantee de facto autonomy. A recognized international legal sovereign will not necessarily be a Westphalian sovereign.

In recent years a number of analysts have used the Westphalian model as a bench mark to assert that the character of the international system is changing in some fundamental ways. Writing of the pre-1950s world, James Rosenau contends that "In that system, legitimate authority was concentrated in the policy-making institutions of states, which interacted with each other on the basis of equality and accepted principles of diplomacy and international law. Their embassies remained inviolable and so did their domestic affairs. Intrusion into such matters were met with protests of violated sovereignty and, not infrequently, with preparations for war. For all practical purposes, the line between domestic and foreign affairs was preserved and clearly understood by all. The norms of the Western state system lodged control over external ties in the state and these were rarely defied and even more rarely revised." Philip Windsor states that "It is fashionable, at present, to suggest that the old Westphalian system of a world of non-interventionist states is on the decline, and that the dangers of growing intervention by different powers in the affairs of other states have been on the increase. The Westphalian system represented some remarkable achievements: the absolute sovereignty of a state rested on a dual basis whereby internal authority was matched by freedom from external interference; and in this way the principle of *cuius regio, eius religio,* codified in the Religious Peace of Augsburg, laid the foundation of the modern states

---

40. Wendt and Friedheim 1996, 245.

system."[41]

The way in which some analysts have understood sovereignty in terms of the Westphalian model is brought out clearly by authors who have studied minority or human rights, because claims about such rights are seen as a contradiction of sovereignty. In one of the most important studies of minority rights in the interwar period C. A. Macartney writes, "The doctrine of state sovereignty does not admit that the domestic policy of any state—the policy which it follows towards its own citizens — can be any concern of any other state." In a more recent study of human rights Forsythe suggests that "The most fundamental point about human rights law is that it establishes a set of rules for all states and all people. It thus seeks to increase world unity and to counteract national separateness (but not necessarily national distinctions). In this sense, the international law of human rights is revolutionary because it contradicts the notion of national sovereignty — that is, that a state can do as it pleases in its own jurisdiction." Writing in the 1990s about the status of minority groups Kay Hailbronner claims that "Modern public international law seems to have broken through the armour of sovereignty." Similarly Brian Hehir has asserted that "In the Westphalian order both state sovereignty and the rule of nonintervention are treated as absolute norms." He then goes on to suggest that this Westphalian system is under an unprecedented level of assault.[42]

Despite these claims about unparalleled change, the most important empirical conclusion of the present study is that the principles associated with both Westphalian and international legal sovereignty have always been violated. Neither Westphalian

---

41. Rosenau 1990, 109; Windsor 1984, 45.

42. Macartney 1934, 296; Forsythe 1983, 4; Hailbronner 1992, 117; Hehir 1995, 6.

nor international legal sovereignty has ever been a stable equilibrium from which rulers had no incentives to deviate. Rather, Westphalian and international legal sovereignty are best understood as examples of organized hypocrisy. At times rulers adhere to conventional norms or rules because it provides them with resources and support (both material and ideational). At other times, rulers have violated the norms, and for the same reasons. If rulers want to stay in power and to promote the security, material, and ideational interests of their constituents, following the conventional practices of Westphalian and international legal sovereignty might or might not be an optimal policy. After the Second World War it was preferable for the rulers of western Europe to sign the European Human Rights Convention, which compromised their Westphalian sovereignty, than to insist that the domestic autonomy of their polities be unconstrained. In the late 1990s it was better for the rulers of China and other states to allow Hong Kong, which did not have juridical independence after its return to China, to enjoy international recognition; Hong Kong continued its participation in or joined international organizations, including the World Trade Organization, whose members denied China itself the right to become a founding member.

In sum, analysts and practitioners have used the term sovereignty in four different and distinct ways. The absence or loss of one kind of sovereignty does not logically imply an erosion of others, even though they may be empirically associated with each other. A state can be recognized, but its authority structures can be de facto subject to external authority or control. It can lose control of transborder movements but still be autonomous.

Rulers have almost universally desired international legal

sovereignty,[43] but this has not meant that they have universally followed the rule of recognizing only juridically autonomous territorial entities. Rulers have recognized entities that lack formal juridical autonomy or even territory, and they have denied recognition to governments that have exercised effective control over the territory of a recognized state. Recognition can be a political act, one designed to support a specific government or legitimate the claims to territorial autonomy of particular rulers, and adherence to the basic principle of international legal sovereignty might, or might not, enhance these purposes.

The tensions between the conventional rule and actual practice have been more severe for Westphalian than international legal sovereignty. Rulers have sometimes invited external actors to compromise the autonomy of their own state. Westphalian sovereignty has also been violated through intervention; more powerful states have coerced their weaker counterparts into altering the domestic institutional arrangements of their polities. Following the rule of Westphalian sovereignty — preserving the de facto autonomy of a territorial political entity — might, or might not, further the interests of rulers.

The international system is complex. Information is imperfect. There are no universal structures that can authoritatively resolve conflicts. Principles and rules can be logically contradictory. Power asymmetries can be high. Widely recognized and endorsed principles will not always promote the interests of rulers. Logics of consequences can trump logics of appropriate-

---

43. There have been cases where rulers have sought to abandon international legal sovereignty. For instance, the leaders of Nicaragua and Guatemala asked to join the United States in the 1840s and the president of Belarus contemplated joining with the Soviet Union in 1990s.

ness. Westphalian and international legal sovereignty, the major concerns of this study, are examples of organized hypocrisy. They are both defined by widely understood rules. Yet, these rules have been compromised, more frequently in the case of Westphalian than international legal sovereignty.

References

Bradford, Ernle, *The Shield and the Sword. The Knights of St. John* (London: Hodder and Stoughton, 1972)

Brierly, J. L., *The Law of Nations: An Introduction to the International Law of Peace*. Edited by Humphrey Waldock (6th ed. New York: Oxford University Press, 1963)

Cerny, Philip G., *The Changing Architecture of Politics: Structur, Agency, and the Future of the State* (London: Sage, 1990)

Crawford, Beverly, *Explaining Defection from International Cooperation: Germany's Unilateral Recognition of Croatia*, in: World Politics 48 (1996), 482-521.

Damrosch, Lori, *Changing Conceptions of Intervention in International Law*, in: *Emerging Norms of Justified Intervention: A Collection of Essays from a Project of the American Academy of Arts and Sciences*, edited by Laura W. Reed and Carl Kaysen (Cambridge, Mass.: American Academy of Arts and Sciences, 1993) 91-110.

Deudney, Daniel H., *The Philadelphian System: Sovereignty, Arms Control, and Balance of Power in the American States-Union*, circa 1787-1861, in: International Organizations 49, 441-473.

Forsythe, David P., *Human Rights and World Politics* (Lincoln: University of Nebraska Press 1983)

Fowler, Michael Ross, and Julie Marie Bunck, *Law, Power, and the Sovereign State: The Evolution and Application of the Concept of Sovereignty* (University Park: Pennsylvania State University Press, 1995)

Garrett, Geoffrey, *Global Markets and National Politics: Collision Course or Virtuous Cycle*, in: International Organization 52 (1998) 787-824.

Hailbronner, Kay, *The Legal Status of Population Groups in a Multinational State under Public International Law*, in: *The Protection of Minorities and Human Rights*, edited by Yoram Dinstein and Mala Tabory (Dordrecht: Martinus Nijhoff, 1992) 117-144.

Hehir, J. Brian, *Intervention: From Theories to Cases*, in: Ethics and International Affairs 9 (1995) 1-14.

Hinsley, F. H., *Sovereignty* (2nd ed. Cambridge: Cambridge University Press, 1986)

Jackson, Robert H., *Quasi-States: Sovereignty, International Relations and the Third World.* (Cambridge: Cambridge University Press, 1990)

Keohane, Robert O., *After Hegemony: Cooperation and Discord in the World Political Economy* (Princeton: Princeton University Press, 1984)

Keohane, Robert O., *Hobbe's Dilemma and Institutional Change in World Politics: Sovereignty in International Society*, in: *Whose World Order? Uneven Globalization and the End of the Cold War* (Hans-Hendrik Holm / Georg Sorensen (eds.) Bolder, Col. 1995, 165-186).

Krasner, Stephen D., *Sovereignty. Organized Hypocrisy.* (Princeton, NJ, 1999, 9-25).

Macartney, Carlile Aylmer, *National States and National Minorities* (Oxford: Oxford University Press, 1934)

Mathews, Jessica Tuchman, *Power Shift*, in: Foreign Affairs 76 (1997) 50-66.

Miller, James Edward, *The United States and Italy, 1940-1950: The Politics and Diplomacy of Stabilization* (Chapel Hill: University of North Carolina Press 1986)

Movsesian, Mark L., *The Persistent Nation State and the Foreign Sovereign Immunities Act*, 18, in: Cardozo Law Revue 1083 (1996)

Obstfeld, M., and A. M. Taylor, *The Great Depressions as a Watershed: International Capital Mobility over the Long Run*. Working Paper No. 5960 (Cambridge, Mass.: National Bureau of Economic Research 1997)

Onuf, Nicholas Greenwood., *Sovereignty: Outline of a Conceptual History*, in: Alternatives 16 (1991) 425-446.

Oppenheim, L., *Oppenheim's International Law*. Edited by Robert Jennings and Arthur Watts, 9th ed. Harlow (Essex: Longman 1992)

Peterson, Edward N., *The American Occupation of Germany: Retreat to Victory* (Detroit: Wayne State University Press 1977)

Peterson, M. J., *Political Use of Recognition: The Influence of the International System*, in: World Politics 34 (1982) 324-352.

——, *Recognition of Governments: Legal Doctrine and State Practice* (New York: St. Martin's Press, 1997)

Rosenau, James, *Turbulence in World Politics: A Theory of*

Change and Continuity (Princeton, N.J.: Princeton University Press 1990)

Shue, Henry, *Eroding Sovereignty: The Advance of Principle*, in: *The Morality of Nationalism*, edited by Robert McKim and Jeff McMahan (New York: Oxford University Press 1997) 340-359.

Skinner, Quentin, *The Foundations of Modern Political Thought*, vol. 2, *The Age of Reformation* (Cambridge: Cambridge University Press 1978)

Strang, David, *Contested Sovereignty: The Social Construction of Colonial Imperialism*, in: *State Sovereignty as a Social Construct*, edited by Thomas Biersteker and Cynthia Weber (Cambridge: Cambridge University Press 1996) 22-49.

Strayer, Joseph R., *On the Medieval Origins of the Modern State* (Princeton, N.J.: Princeton University Press 1970)

Sugden, Robert, *Spontaneous Order*, in: Journal of Economic Perspectives 3 (1989) 85-97.

Thomas, Ann, and A. J. Thomas, *Non Intervention: The Law and Its Import in the Americas* (Dallas: Southern Methodist University Press, 1956)

Thomson, Janice E., *State Sovereignty in International Relations: Bridging the Gap between Theory and Empirical Research*, in: International Studies Quarterly 39 (1995) 213-233.

Thomson, Janice E., and Stephen D. Krasner, *Global Transactions and the Consolidation of Sovereignty*, in: *Global Changes and Theoretical Challenges: Approaches to World Politics for the 1990s*, edited by E. O. Czempiel and J. N. Rosenau (Lexington, Mass.: D.C.Heath.1989) 195-219.

Vattel, Emer de., *The Law of Nations; or, Principles of the Law of*

Nature, applied to the Conduct and Affairs of Nations and Sovereigns. From the new edition translated by Joseph Chitty, (Philadelphia: T. & J. W. Johnson, Law Booksellers 1852)

Weiler, Joseph H. H., *The Transformation of Europe*, in: Yale Law Journal 100 (1991) 2403-2483.

Wendt, Alexander, *Anarchy Is What States Make of It: The Social Construction of State Politics*, in: International Organization 46 (1992) 391-425.

Wendt, Alexander, and Daniel Friedheim, *Hierarchy under Anarchy: Informal Empire and the East German State*, in: *State Sovereignty as a Social Construct*, edited by Thomas Biersteker and Cynthia Weber (Cambridge: Cambridge University Press 1996) 240-272.

Williamson, Jeffrey, *Globalization and the Labor Market: Using History to Inform Policy*, (Milan: Lezioni Raffaele Mattioli, Banca Commerciale Italiana, Università Commerciale Luigi Bocconi,1996)

Windsor, Philip, *Superpower Intervention*, in: *Intervention in World Politics*, edited by Hedley Bull (Oxford: Clarendon Press 1984) 45-65.

Wriston, Walter, *Bits, Bytes, and Diplomacy*, in: Foreign Affairs 76 (1997) 172-182.

Mastering Globalization:
State-Building and Sovereignty in the EU

Penny Gill

Europeans are engaged in a wide-ranging argument about the future of the European Union: will the euro lead to further social and political integration? Will member state sovereignty be preserved or diluted by further integration? Is democratization even possible at the level of the EU's complex processes of decision-making? And how can the requirements of democracy be meshed with the requirements of making complex public policy in an intensely competitive global environment? It is a moment rich in ambiguities for many European participants.

The European Community, in its first incarnation as the European Coal and Steel Community, was intended to make impossible another deadly continental war. Germany's heavy industries were harnessed by the supra-national regulation of the ECSC, in what would become the seed of the huge spreading tree of European organizations today.[1] But somewhere, a second and deeply entrenched motive had a greater and greater impact, perhaps as it became increasingly clear that the UK, with its instinctive reliance on the Atlantic connection, would not commit itself to a

---

1. An excellent introduction to the EU and its history is Desmond Dinan, Ever Closer Union (Boulder, 1999). A highly critical view is developed by John Laughland, The Tainted Source: The Undemocratic Origins of the European Idea (London, 1997).

leadership role inside Europe.[2] The new motive was to compete effectively with that most difficult ally and partner, the United States. The EEC initially had been a defensive economic community, which built a protective wall of common tariffs against "overly competitive" imports. Later it would develop a more offensive strategy and use the EU to create a single market in goods, services, labor and capital. The intent was clear: to strengthen productivity, improve economic growth, stimulate research and development, expand job creation, support exports, and establish stable currencies. Since then both globalization and the structural changes in the region resulting from the collapse of the USSR have significantly changed the environment and the pressing issues facing the EU.

My question in this essay is whether globalization has also become one of those forces maintaining pressure towards more and more integration in Europe, both horizontally and vertically. In some ways, it seems to me, the Europeans find themselves in a very idiosyncratic process of state formation. A state is forming without much attention to citizens, something perhaps not seen since the Renaissance. Raising the questions about globalization and its implications for European integration should give us a better understanding of state sovereignty and, eventually, state formation in contemporary Europe.

First, I will summarize very briefly several concepts of globalization. In the second section I will discuss globalization in Europe and some of its main characteristics. Sections III and IV explore several aspects of the huge discussion underway among academics and political activists about sovereignty and state building in Europe. Finally, in the last section I will attempt a brief

---

2. Hugo Young, This Blessed Plot: Britain and Europe from Churchill to Blair (London, 1998).

summary of the situation today and suggest some possible implications for both integration and democratization in Europe.

1. Globalization: The Contemporary Phenomenon

In the last several years the term "globalization" seems to have acquired both fame and notoriety in the mass media as well as become a ripe field for a burgeoning academic industry. The most common view (Thomas Friedman, for example) argues that "globalization" refers to the rapidly increasing dispersion and integration of free market capitalism, under the twin stimuli of the unprecedently rapid development of information technology and the resultant rapid pace and ease of international capital flows.[3] It is not clear yet how these three dimensions might be related to each other, or even if their simultaneous occurrence is an odd historical coincidence or evidence they are facets of a single phenomenon. What startles most observers is the intensity of the integrative processes, the depth of change (in the sense of how deep into the "normally" protected arenas of domestic policy) the speed of the change, and states' inability to defend themselves or to erect any meaningful barriers against globalization. State boundaries become more porous by the week.

The first motor of globalization is computers and the cybernetic transformation of our world. When we first met the room-

---

3. Thomas Friedman argues that globalization, with its integration of capital, technology, and information around the world and across national borders, is the best description of the new international system. The Lexus and the Olive Tree (New York, 1999.) Roland Axtmann, ed., Globalization and Europe: Theoretical and Empirical Investigations (London, 1998) is a useful collection of more analytical essays.

sized mainframe computer forty years ago, it was a powerful new tool for finding patterns in large quantities of data. Students of politics also recognized a compelling metaphor for how complex societies and polities process information and make decisions. Probably no one recognized the world itself had been shrunk to the realm of milliseconds, the speed at which images, messages, data, or ultimately, capital could speed round the globe. In this frame, the world is indeed wrapped up in a web that really none can escape. Linked mobile phones, wireless technology, small computers, and the Web are eroding the ability of states to control the flow of information or to maintain boundaries more significantly than any event since Admiral Perry sailed into Japan's harbor in 1854. We may or may not be brave, but there is no real escape from this very new world.

    The second dimension of our emerging understanding of globalization is the flow of capital in and out of global markets, often at the speed of an e-mail message. That capital seems to seek out new markets with a kind of urgency, a sign perhaps of the extraordinary growth in the huge powerhouse economies of the US and Europe. New host markets envision capital flowing in as the long awaited opportunity for rapid economic development that will allow them to leap-frog out of the primary economy to which they have been confined for two centuries. Their hope is that the new capital will also bring job creation, new opportunities for trade and earning hard currencies, and substantial improvement in domestic infrastructure and local economic performance.

    The immediate price that "emerging economies" must pay up front, of course, is that their domestic markets must open themselves to foreign capital. Eventually that will include making the standards and practices of legal, property, financial, and currency regulatory institutions acceptable to the owners of this new capital. The risks are huge. Foreign investment may be too meager or ill directed. Local infrastructure may be unable to function adequately, with profound implications for domestic politics and social well being. A currency can collapse overnight, as soft money is pulled out of an economy without warning. The IMF and the World Bank will arrive, with their adjustment policies and conditions for a bail out.

Again, as in the case of information technology, it is extremely difficult for a state to protect itself from unwanted or potentially disruptive capital flows. The price is usually too high: severely restricted foreign investment, closed export markets, and sharply reduced economic performance. Even China has begun to open up sectors of its giant economy to foreign investment, while hoping to fence it in inside one relatively small "free trade" area. Most analysts think eventually even that fire wall will become so porous as to be nearly symbolic; the long term implications of that are impossible to predict, but political and social change will be inescapable.

The new investments, regardless of the limits on access to domestic markets (for example, limits on foreign ownership, reserved sectors, and currency and banking controls), seem often to be accompanied by some new values as well. We commonly call this package "liberal democracy" or "free market capitalism". Free competition and unregulated markets are often accompanied by the desire for more individual freedom, the rudiments of civil society, support for the rule of law (especially that undergirding private property and the enforceability of contracts), and attempts to increase the democratic accountability of government - profound challenges to regimes like China, Saudi Arabia, or Cuba.

Critics note the spread of other values and cultural practices wrapped in the language of liberalism or liberal democracy, and often name it "Americanization", with its connotation of manipulative consumerism, hyper-individualism, and the pursuit of individual gain above all other social and community values. Local residents complain of invasions by American cultural icons, film, and pop music, sensualism, anti-family practices, and feminist and other sex/gender depravities. They often fear secularization and the loss of traditional culture.

This perception of globalization as the homogenization of dominant cultural and social values, held by articulate and influential elites around the world, can unleash powerful and aggressive forces, from a simple ethnic national revival to Jihad in all its forms.[4] But this may also be a cause of the current "Third Wave" of democratization on every continent, as groups rise to respond to the economic and cultural "invasions". We see new grass roots organizations and social movements, demands for more environmental protection, discussion of language requirements for citizenship, urgent calls for devolution, and calls for protection from the rigors of new treaties mandating lower tariffs and free trade.

This first, common view of globalization focuses on the first world/third world aspect of capital flows and globalization. In addition, within the first world we must note the remarkable pace of privatization of huge public sector enterprises and the mergers and takeovers that result in significant corporate consolidation. We are left to wonder if these several dimensions of what we loosely denote as globalization - 1) the rapid emergence of a global market with seemingly inexorable capacities for capitalist/free market expansion, 2) cultural and social values and practices embraced by increasing segments of the global population, and 3) the marked

---

4. Benjamin Barber, Jihad vs. McWorld: How Globalism and Tribalism are Reshaping the World (New York, 1995). Mary Kaldor raises some interesting questions in "Cosmopolitanism Versus Nationalism: The New Divide", in Richard Caplan and John Feffer, eds., Europe's New Nationalism (Oxford, 1996), pp. 42-58.

pressures toward increasing democratization - the third wave - in new and previously undemocratic regions of the world are in truth a single process of nearly unimaginable complexity? Or is it something less, not more, than the sum of its parts?

Globalization can also be usefully conceptualized as the gradual construction of and expansion of an inter-statal system.[5] The modern international system has become an expanding system of states that recognize each other as states, whose regimes may relate to one another in a variety of ways (that is, through cooperation, threat, war, invasion, and such). This is truly a global event; with the possible exception of small parts of Africa, most of the world's population now live within the boundaries of a modern state. It is important to remember this is an historical event, not just the "normal state of affairs".

In addition to the expansion of information technology with its making possible a global capital market or the convergence of cultural values and themes, analysts have suggested that globalization really refers to a new form of hyper-imperialism, with even more significant arenas of the third world or southern hemisphere now controlled by specific economic interests based in the first world. This would be a new version of a very old history. The moment when Europeans first explored and then developed systems to exploit natural resources in regions outside their continent would be the real start of what we now recognize as globalization. The resources, productive capacities, and people of North and South America, Africa, and Asia, in an extraordinary variety of means, were brought within the orbits of Europeans prepared to use them, abuse them, or improve them. Regardless of the motive or the method, much of the world's population that had lived in the

---

5. See Jean Houbert, "Decolonization in Globalization", in Axtmann, ed., Globalization and Europe, pp. 43-58.

fullness of their own small communities were forced into relationships with a part of the world nearly unknown before.

By the end of the 1960's, virtually all these territories had constructed their own states, often having fought for their independence. That is not to imply that with formal independence came economic or cultural autonomy. Along with the deep penetration of American and European economic forces into the former colonial world - one direction of globalization - came another in the reverse direction: a steady flow of immigrants, refugees, and asylum seekers into European and American societies. It is no real surprise to Americans any more to find a Thai restaurant in their neighborhood, but the northern European reactions to discovering they are living in increasingly multi-cultural societies - even if not yet recognized as multi national states - are fueling a significant type of resistance to what is perceived as the forces of globalization.

We must describe a very complex and multi-layered set of patterns to grasp the political consequences of rapid globalization. We should not be so perplexed, for example, to find Europeans building a new neighborhood ghetto with hastily erected walls for Roma or to watch a right wing political party whose leader seems to have praised aspects of the Third Reich become the junior partner of a parliamentary coalition and cabinet. We do not seem able to understand powerful disintegrative forces in the Balkans. We appear paralyzed, unable to act appropriately or effectively, in the face of these disintegrative pressures. Are these signs of social conflict and even national disintegration somehow sui generis, on one hand, or indicative of an essential primitiveness of peripheral ethnic politics in Europe in a region not amenable to the advantages of this new post-modern economy and state system? I would argue that we can best understand these forces as stimulated by and a powerful response to the pressures of globalization.

2. Globalization in Europe

Is it necessary to offer a description of the signs of globalization in Europe today? We can all point to the accomplishments of the EU: the creation of a single market, with a single regulatory authority; the creation of the euro and the European Central Bank and the deepening integration of a single monetary policy; the standardization of communication protocols facilitating explosive growth in information technology; an emerging preference for a single, common second language; multiplying cross-national mergers; consolidation of banking, transportation, and financial markets; and students routinely studying "abroad," if that is even the correct word anymore. Beyond the fifteen, Central Europeans, free to choose their own futures since the fall of the Wall, press towards Brussels.

It is common to consider Europeans as recipients or even victims of globalizing pressures, and to many Europeans, especially those outside the main decision-making centers of Brussels and the national capitals, EU regulations and the pressures of globalization seem one and the same. There is another way to frame this question: we could think of the EU as a way to master the apparent disadvantages of globalization. This, I will argue, opens up a new way to think about sovereignty and sovereign states.[6]

First, economic integration, especially the creation of a single market and the systematic removal of hindrances to competi-

---

6. How economic forces shape or even determine political events is of course an old argument, one no less intense today. For example, see John Dunn, ed., The Economic Limits to Modern Politics (Cambridge, 1990); Herbert Kitschelt, Peter Lange, Gary Marks, and John D. Stephens, eds., Continuity and Change in Contemporary Capitalism (Cambridge, 1999); and Andrew Moravcsik, The Choice for Europe (Ithaca, New York), 1998.

tion within Europe, has been a powerful influence on the restructuring of the European economies. It has prepared the ground for future economic growth, strengthened Europe's ability to protect itself against incursions from US and multi-national corporations, and even provided an authoritative representative to argue more successfully against US positions in global trade negotiations. By improving productivity in its own economies, the EU prepares itself and the member states to gain competitive advantages in global markets. What began in part as a defensive measure against US economic pressure becomes in turn its own mechanism for passing globalizing pressures on to third world countries in the emerging global markets.

The second aspect of how the EU has become a powerful tool to master the problems of globalization is how it has strengthened the hands of those in each member state who wished to rein in national social budgets, limit the benefits of the social welfare systems, and push for a more conservative fiscal policy. The desire to meet the convergence criteria for joining the euro, for example, assisted national policy makers who embraced the long term goals of reducing deficit financing, limiting job protections, placing new limits on unemployment compensation, and rationing more carefully a whole host of social payments. The EU could be blamed at an electoral/populist moment, but the budget-disciplining vote could still carry in the parliament. The EU seems to provide a larger context within which issues framed in new ways can loosen old alliances and habits of thought commonplace in the post-war systems of corporative compromise and social stability.[7]

---

7. Martin Rhodes, "The Welfare State: Internal Challenges, External Constraints", in Rhodes, Paul Heywood, and Vincent Wright, eds., Developments in West European Politics (New York, 1997), pp. 57-74.

The third aspect of this is of particular interest. I think the EU has become a way to reinforce the legitimacy of national regimes. Paradoxically, from the point of view of member state political elites, it can be a very shrewd strategy to facilitate increasing integration in the EU, even if it requires surrendering some dimensions of sovereign authority for certain areas of public policy, both economic and even political. The intention is to shore up weakening national political legitimacy. But it is a strategy that must be pursued silently, even verbally disavowed whenever possible.

The usual post-war way of increasing legitimacy had been for the national government to deliver economic security and social peace via the creation of the welfare state, with its intricate webs of benefits, guarantees, and consensus politics. The oil crisis of 1973 initiated a steady weakening of these basic social arrangements, accompanied by rising inflation, rising unemployment, decreasing productivity with increasing global competition, and even tax resistance.[8]

Shifting some sovereign powers to the EU enabled it to enhance the national economic performance of member states, reduce regional conflict, and strengthen the European role in international affairs. Elites seem to have created the common currency especially to try to maximize their leverage on global economic pressures well beyond the control of any one state. Did they also intend the euro to become a way to strengthen European defenses against

---

8. For a fuller discussion of the modern state and its shifting sources of legitimacy, see G. Poggi, The Development of the Modern State (Stanford, Calif., 1978). Kenneth H. F. Dyson tracks a range of conceptualizations of the modern state and sovereignty in various European political traditions in The State Tradition in Western Europe: A Study of an Idea and Institution (New York, 1980).

the American hegemon? In any event, each new arena of EU activity reduces the demands upon national regimes and increases their effectiveness in other realms of public policy.

In contrast to this view, many critics conceptualize the EU/member state relationship as a zero sum game and see further integration in Europe as fundamentally destructive of nation-state sovereignty. It is a central debate currently in the UK, Austria, Norway, and Switzerland, for example, but it is part of the domestic debate in most of the member states.

3. Globalization and Sovereignty

As a function of recognition within the inter-state system, sovereignty is the capacity of a state to do as it wishes within its own territorial boundaries, without hindrance from other states, a capacity recognized by other sovereign states. Only a state can claim this capacity for autonomous decision-making, but at a practical level, that claim depends upon the assent of the international or inter-statal system operative in the historical moment and in that geographic region.

This seems to suggest that sovereignty might in fact be rather fluid and potentially indeterminate, more a consequence of a state's claims to autonomy in certain sectors and the responses (or, more critically, the non-responses) of neighbor states. Rather than a simple dichotomous category (sovereign/not sovereign), a more useful metaphor might be that of an elaborate dance or masque, in which each dancer bows deferentially to the claims of others, that he too may receive the deep salute of mutual recognition.[9]

The first fundamental claim of a sovereign state is to a monopoly of power within its own borders. Let me point to two contemporary examples: Russia claims sovereignty over the territory of Chechnya. Russia's inability to subdue the Chechyn separatists does not seriously weaken its claim, at least in the short run, so long as neighbor states and relevant globally powerful states choose not to contest Russia's territorial claim.

If Russia were to advance similar claims or pursue a similar military action in Estonia, for example, it is unlikely that the international system would just fidget and keep its mouth shut. The two cases differ significantly, of course: historically, Chechnya and Estonia have had very different relations with their powerful neighbor; domestic political identities and traditions differ significantly; the regional neighborhoods carry different salience for regional power brokers; and all this contributes to very different evaluations of national interest by some very powerful European and North American states. The fundamental claim of a sovereign state, then, is the right to maintain its own boundaries, and from it flow other dimensions of the exercise of sovereign power.[10]

Recent events in the Balkans suggest a new limit on the conventional system of state sovereignty in the west: Yugoslavia, a sovereign state, now faces significant restrictions when dealing

---

9. Thomas J. Biersteker, "Locating the Emerging European Polity: Beyond States or State?", in Jeffrey J. Anderson, ed., Regional Integration and Democracy (Boulder, 1999), pp. 21-44.

10. I do not have space to discuss this here, but one would want to consider next how the state provides a "site" for a potentially provocative argument about who comprises this state, with its self-claimed right to maintain its own boundaries and itself.

with Kosovo, citizens in its own territory. Even though the relevant neighbor states and the US rejected the Kosovo demand for its own sovereign state, they insisted there were still limits to the actions the Yugoslavia government could take against its own civilian population. Forced evacuation, wide scale attack, and assaults on civilians of that very state seem no longer to be permissible under the cloak of domestic sovereignty. Iraqi attacks on its Kurdish population provide a similar example. This seems to be part of a continuing development in international law and practice in the last century. We note, for example, the European Court of Human Rights, the international tribunals, developing practices at the UN and other international organizations, and the increasing willingness of powerful states to intervene in situations of massive violations of human rights within the accepted territorial boundaries of a recognized sovereign state. No longer, then, if ever, can a state exercise full and undiluted sovereignty without possible response from the international community. Afghanistan, Myanmar, Yugoslavia, and Iraq each has had its claims to its exercise of sovereign powers rejected at least in part by other states.

I have considered sovereignty as a characteristic of states within the global state system; sovereignty is also the capacity of a state to act, to pursue its own foreign and domestic policies. This includes, for example, the essential activities of a state: maintaining civil order and justice (as in laws, police, courts, and systems of punishment); providing for security and defense; and because all of this must be paid for, regulating economic activity (especially markets, trade, currency, property law, and contracts) and collecting taxes.

This is precisely why the EU is such a fascinating laboratory for those who wish to understand how sovereignty really "works" in the post-modern world. In many significant areas of public policy, member states have shifted some ultimate authority to the EU. As soon as we drop down to an analytic level that allows us to watch concrete policy making, we see sovereignty in a very different light. It is no longer a single indivisible characteristic, like virginity. Sovereignty is fluid, divisible, and vulnerable to shifts in both the domestic and the international environments. Sometimes it seems remarkably subtle and difficult even to track, except in rare cases where decision-making is transparent and implementation visible and successful. A loss of sovereignty in one arena does not necessarily mean it has been weakened in any other.

Three examples of thousands available illustrate this: 1) The Cassis case, in which the European Court of Justice essentially claimed that EU treaties and the court's interpretations of them had legal precedence over member state law and practice. 2) The Maastricht Treaty, which established the European Central Bank, established the euro, and laid out the criteria and the evaluation processes for acceding to the common currency. 3) The policies arising out of the British beef controversy, beginning with the EU's embargo of British beef. This eventually became a political crisis of some significance: could the EU impose a settlement on a trade battle between two member states? Where is the boundary between protectionism, which is not allowed, and the protection of the health and safety of a member state's citizens, which is allowed? What are the limits of the Commission's authority in such matters, and will the Court enforce its judgments?

To put the matter even more bluntly: have the member states lost sovereign control of borders, import regulations, health and safety provisions, or even the identity of their national beverages? Did the member states lose their sovereign control over fiscal policy and their ability to manage national debt or money supply? Did citizens lose their ability to determine the social provisions of national budgets, when states agreed to accept the convergence criteria for joining the euro?

Only part of the answer to each question is "yes". For example, the treaty that established the European Central Bank was adopted after a complex process of discussion, negotiation, and ultimately ratification by each member state. A sovereign state can "give away" some of its authority to a new institution, such as the UN, NATO, or the WTO. It may also retain the right of veto or non-compliance, as in some inter-governmental decision-making aspects of the EU.

Is it not also possible to say without contradiction that the ECJ expresses the sovereignty of the EU member states, at the same time that it dilutes the full exercise of national autonomy in judicial matters? The several US states, associated under the relatively loose framework of the Articles of Confederation, did something quite similar when they "gave" certain powers to a new federal government.[11] I do not think these are simply semantic solutions to otherwise very difficult political theoretical problems. A stereoptic view of sovereignty includes both the level of inter-statal relations and the exercise of a fluid and divisible authority in multiple areas of public policy, at the intra-state level. Policy effectiveness may well be enhanced for a state, especially in the context of intense globalization pressures, by "pooling" sovereign authority and creating a new level of decision-making. The image that comes to mind is "nesting dolls", in which ultimate authority might be at any one of several levels: control of trade policy may best be accomplished by using a regional (EU) authority, while educational and cultural policy may be assigned to sub-national levels. The flexibility intended by the notion of "subsidiarity" could be usefully marshalled as a conceptual device to understand how state sovereignty might be distributed among two or more levels of

---

11. See Gordon S. Wood's magisterial account of this process: The Creation of the American Republic, 1776-1787 (Chapel Hill, 1998).

decision-making. Because such a distribution can engender significant political and juridical disputes, this would seem to require something resembling a constitution.

To summarize, sovereignty can be shifted, pooled, dispersed, and even augmented through complex political strategies to achieve greater regime efficacy, better responsiveness to difficult international/global environments, and more skillful defenses against the most destructive dimensions of globalization. The fifteen member states are creating a new level of sovereign authority in Europe precisely to reinforce the political and policy making effectiveness of each state.

4. The EU: Talk Shops or a proto-State?

If the Europeans are really creating a new level of sovereign authority, is it useful to think of it as the kernel of a new Europe-wide state? It is not a simple question, since NATO, the Hague Court, and the WTO seem also to be vehicles of member states' sovereign powers, as established by treaty. We would never imagine the UN or NATO to be a proto-state. The European Court of Justice, the euro, and the European Central Bank certainly are "recipient" institutions, whose authority to act within some carefully delimited boundaries is prescribed by treaty. This may suggest the seeds of state-hood at the regional level are present. Whether and how they will be developed is a vexing and difficult question facing both the EU and its students right now.

The classic distinction used by both framers and analysts of the several European organizations and "communities" - that between inter-governmental and supra-national (a distinction quite astonishing in its mixing of conceptual categories) – is helpful, but perhaps not as useful as it once was. I would like to suggest two criteria that I think help us focus better: 1) So long as the dominant form of decision-making requires unanimity or concensus among participants - rather than some form of conflict-resolving procedure like majority voting, qualified majority voting, weighted pluralities, or such - that body is not a state. 2) If any member state can formally opt out, or informally choose to ignore, a decision made according to normal procedure, or refuse to fund its share of an activity, it is not yet a state. Mad cow disease and foot and mouth disease may well offer us an unfortunate arena in which to study the relative power of the Commission and the member state governments, and perhaps the ultimate authority of ECJ as well.

The EU's authority to make binding policy is most obvious in the European Court of Justice and its claims both that the treaties "trump" domestic laws and that it has the legal authority to interpret the treaties.[12] In this way the treaties function very similarly to a founding constitution, with which legislation and practices must align themselves in the enumerated areas. The most far-reaching competencies of the court are those directing the achievement of a single market; more and more barriers to competition are being removed. Because of their powerful consequences for competitive advantages and disadvantages in a market with the free mobility of goods, service, capital, and labor, the social policies in the member states seem also to be inching towards greater alignment with each other.

The accomplishment of the single market, largely the work of the Commission over several decades, has resulted in a signifi-

---

12. For more on the European Court of Justice, see Dinan, Closer Union, ch. 15; K. Alter, "The Making of a Supranational Rule of Law: The Battle for Supremacy", in Ronald Tiersky, ed., Europe Today (Boulder, 1999), pp. 305-336; and Ms. Shapiro, "The European Court of Justice", in Alberta Sbragia, ed., Euro-Politics (Washington, 1992), pp. 123-156.

cant shift of decision-making from national legislatures to the EU. The product of this, the "acquis", the mountain of regulations and procedures the aspirant EU members are struggling to adopt and implement, now frames much of the decision-making reach of European parliaments. Eighty percent of normal legislation is now shaped by EU regulations. Examples are legion: gender equality in the workplace, environmental regulations, safety standards in the workplace, product standards, and competition policy, to name just a few.[13]

The second significant arena of shifted sovereign authority is the common currency.[14] Establishing the new European Central Bank and the euro required a quite remarkable self discipline on the part of member state governments to meet the convergence criteria. Even those that did not in the end choose to join the common currency tried to comply with the economic, fiscal, and monetary targets. Certainly transfering state control of monetary policy to another body is a sign of redistributed sovereign authority and a diminution of member state authority, even if in actual practice it results in enhanced competence and effectiveness at reaching specific economic goals. Some of those goals are relatively obvious - increased job creation, controlled inflation, im-

---

13. In addition to works cited above, see H. Wallace and H. Wallace, eds., Policy-Making in the European Union; Richard Falk and Tamas Szentes, eds., A New Europe in the Changing Global System (Tokyo, 1997); Jeremy J. Richardson, ed., European Union: Power and Decision Making (London, 1996); and Jack Hayward and Edward C. Page, eds., Governing the New Europe (Durham, N.C., 1995); among others.

14. For a critical discussion of the euro, see Bernard H. Moss and Jonathan Michie, eds., The Single European Currency in National Perspective, and E. Jones, "The Politics of the EMU", in Tiersky, ed., Europe Today, pp. 273-304.

proved productivity, and expanding exports. It seems likely, as mentioned earlier, also to be a defensive move against the pressures arising from the intensifying global competitive pressures facing the inflexible and relatively unproductive economies of western Europe.

In addition to the Bank and the Court, the most supranational dimensions of the EU (and thus the best evidence of the emergence of the outlines of a new or a new kind of state), is the Commission. Some have argued that the European Parliament and the Council provide a primitive form of proto-bicameral legislative institutions for a federal Europe, some time in the future. The EP at this date has no significant powers to make policy. Its main task is to consider proposals introduced by the Commission, and it cannot yet generate new or even much amend potential legislation. The Council operates largely as the intergovernmental body it was originally meant to be, especially in the last several years, when it has once again taken the central leadership role. It is the Council - the gathered heads of government and the various groupings of ministers by portfolio - who have pursued the single currency. It is the same group struggling now with the second pillar in the EU, trying to establish a standing European defense and military force. It is the Council that is wrestling with the institutional changes that everyone agrees must be worked out before new members are allowed to approach the hallowed gates of Brussels. And it will be in the Council that the real decisions, certainly political as much as economic/technical, that will determine when the central European states will be admitted.

Much has been written about the tensions between the federalists and the inter-governmentalists. In practical terms, this may be one of the most persistent political divides within Europe and the EU. Much depends, of course, on which part of the EU we look at when we ask questions about national sovereignty, for the

EU, if anything, is a heterogeneous collection of institutions, councils, committees, and talk-shops. Most are available for a wide variety of uses by ministers and EU civil servants. We should remind ourselves to be skeptical of simple claims, for example, that the Council is always characterized by inter-governmental decision-making, the Commission by supra-national decision-making.

This is further complicated because much decision-making is invisible or even off the record. It is nearly impossible to determine when true unanimity was unreachable, or what was the political meaning of the decision to use or not use qualified majority voting (QMV). National political elites may choose for tactical reasons to bounce a decision up to the EU or to hide behind a particular treaty provision or even a particular alignment of votes within the Council. Quid pro quos and complex compromises negotiated by political leaders are often aggregated into huge legislative "packages" sensitive to domestic electoral pressures across member state borders, in ways that make interpreting any particular vote quite difficult.

The distinctions between inter-governmental and supra-national may be much more blurred than we realize, and it is certainly more complex than simply referring to the site of the decision, for example, the Council or the European Parliament. It is more than just a bit of procedural sloppiness on the part of the Eurocrats, I suspect, but rather a growing grey area within which significant areas of policy have been identified and new initatives crafted.

In short, I am more inclined to think that as the real work of the EU actually proceeds, an entirely new kind of structure is being constructed, not necessarily by design, but more as the outcome of innumerable smaller policy decisions and compromises. This "new thing" is actually a multi-level system of policy making authority with multiple sets of procedures and decision-making rules.[15] As of today, there is no definite map of procedures for resolving conflicts among the multiple decision-making bodies. Many had hoped the recently released draft constitution (June 2003) would provide a clear map of institutional responsibilities and demarcate new interrelationships in policy making. But the 200 pages document seems more an expression of current practice than a corrective. The sovereignty of the member states is dispersed among different levels to various decision-making institutions, each with its own decision-making rules, reflecting specific pieces of four major treaties. The particular configuration operative in any one instance actually varies for the area of policy, the particular participants, and the extremely complex mixture of domestic political pressures on multiple participants.

How might we assess the situation today? In part through persistent strategic planning and implementation and in part the outcome of messy and unpredictable "pull and tug" behind the scenes, member states have constructed not a simple new state called the EU or the United States of Europe. During more than fifty years of deals, compromises, horse trading, petulant fits by heads of government, and slogging away by thousands of civil servants, they have built the EU that was politically possible. Everyone agrees it is unwieldy and slow to act and that responses are often too little, too late. EU policy makers whom I interviewed in the summer of 1999 without exception pointed to their inability to respond adequately and in a timely fashion to the disintegration

---

15. Elizabeth Pond argues that this "new thing" is peculiar to Europe. "The emerging European governance has nothing to do with a 'new world order.' It is a 'postmodern,' postnational island - albeit a large one - in a world that consists primarily of 'modern' nation-states (like China, Iran, and the United States) and still 'premodern' chaos . . . ." The Rebirth of Europe (Washington, 1999), p. 204.

in the former Yugoslavia as a powerful "wake-up call" to these institutional and procedural difficulties.

A simple balance sheet might look like this:
- Legal systems operate within a general framework of EU law that has been expanded by European Court of Justice's interpretations of the treaties.
- Currency and monetary policy are steered by the ECB and its independent bank regulators.
- A single market in goods, services, labor, and capital has largely been achived. Trade, tariffs, competition policies, and further efforts at removing hindrances to the operation of a single market are monitored by the Commission, which has regulatory powers. There is access to several levels of redress, including the ECJ.
- Both the Commission and the European Court of Human Rights have become powerful instruments for protecting human rights, preventing discrimination on the basis of ethnic identity, gender, or citizenship. Citizens have gained the right to sue their governments in the Court for violation of their human rights.
- The Schengen Agreement establishes a single external border, drops all internal border controls, and should lead to better coordination of asylum, immigration, naturalization, and citizenship policies.
- The determination of citizenship and territory - who is in and who is out - probably the most fundamental exercise of sovereign authority, is blurred now by the free movement of EU citizens within the EU and the nearly common external border created by the Schengen Agreement. In addition, since 1989 the pressures associated with the expansion of the EU are mounting. Although the Commission and the Council some-

times seem to tug in different directions, the technical judgments of the Commission will shape the ultimate decision that must be made by the heads of government. This will require significant reforms of decision-making in EU institutions, most likely in the direction of further integration. The euro, the social agenda, and agricultural support policies require more attention, as do certain aspects of taxation and regulation of financial and security exchanges.
- Europeans are working to implement the two new pillars agreed to at Maastricht - cooperation in justice and domestic police work and establishing a common security and defense capability.

These are close to a list of the major, if not all of the essential, tasks of a modern state. Providing predictable sources of revenue for the central government/monarch, in order to make an army possible, and to pursue war as necessary and/or desirable was the germ of the modern state as we have come to know it. Stable systems were constructed to link regional elites to the center, while neutralizing their abilities to disrupt or oppose the new power centers at the renaissance court. Cascades of authority ultimately penetrated every corner of the countryside, bringing in its train more linguistic uniformity, regulation of local markets, and control of trade.

One major purpose of early modern state formation was to better equip the king and his followers to fight his enemies. Some enemies were undoubtedly close at hand, but others fueled the epochal struggles between France and England, the fight for naval supremacy, the struggle for colonial territories, and the long battle between Christian and Moslem.

States, as we know them today, were "invented" by elites as effective ways to increase their own control of finance, arms, and territory. These appeared to be short term goals, larded with self interest on behalf of survival in a dangerous world. In exchange for loans, gold, and men, regional elites (feudal lords in most cases) demanded and got councils, a share in decisions, and assistance with providing local law and order.[16]

Isn't this what we are looking at in Europe today? Elites take steps to strengthen their control of financial and human resources to help them better compete with a persistent and powerful opponent. The threat is large, as are the stakes of the competition. The new ways of doing things tend to centralize resources, so as to better deploy them in the critical battle: to control one's own fate, especially economic; to secure access to traditional markets; and to penetrate further into new global markets. The opponent is the US and her awesome fecundity at technological innovation and ruthless expansion in the global markets of goods, services, and capital.

As in the sixteenth and seventeen centuries, EU state formation is elite-driven and outwardly focused. There are no citizens here, as there were none then. Neither is there any deep concern about citizen participation or the ultimate sovereignty of the constituent "demos". Except for persistent critical voices from intellectuals, there is little pursuit of democratic accountability, responsible European citizenship, or social justice.[17] The task of

---

16. Martin van Creveld's The Rise and Decline of the State (Cambridge, 1999) is an excellent survey of the history of the modern state in the west. Charles Tilly provides a complex analysis of the same subject in Coercion, Capital, and European States, AD 990 - 1990 (Oxford, 1990).

17. Claus Offe's work is important here, for example, "The Democratic Welfare State in an Integrating Europe", in Michael Th. Greven and Louis W. Pauly, eds., Democracy Beyond the State: The European Dilemma and the Emerging Global Order (Boulder, 2000), pp. 63-90.

legitimation is left to others, perhaps the next generation, except for the frequent reminder that the EU has made Europe a peaceful and increasingly prosperous continent.

If we think of globalization as a very recent phenomenon, largely created by information technology, rapidly expanding global capital markets, and the spread of certain cultural values and practices, we would be correct to consider the EU first a defensive and then an offensive European strategy to protect their economies and societies from US-based competitive pressure. In that sense, the EU is both a response to and an intensifier of globalizing processes in the world. If we think of globalization in its cultural dimension, we might also see the EU as a powerful threat to local and national European identities, as many Europeans also do.

We might also think of globalization as a characteristic of modernity, first visible during the great explorations of the sixteenth and seventeenth centuries, the scramble among the Europeans to colonize great swathes of the other four continents in the eighteenth and nineteenth centuries, and then the spread of capitalist economic systems through a variety of imperial networks in the nineteenth and twentieth centuries. This shifts our understanding of the connections between globalization and European integration since World War II. On the one hand, the institutions of the new Europe seem to be a self-conscious attempt to give form to a united continent, but in a form not imposed by war and conquest. A voluntary, law-based Europe-wide organization then can not only keep the peace and promote social democracy, but it would cease to threaten the peoples of the former colonial worlds. Democracy, stability, and economic development in the third world or in the southern hemisphere then could best be supported by a democratic and stable Europe at peace with itself. In this way of thinking, an integrated Europe tending to its own business would be the best way to break the patterns of the old globalizing systems of colonialism and imperialism.

Is this a fully democratic Europe? Will such a new Europe be able to protect its twentieth-century commitments to social justice and the welfare states? Or, to put it more baldly, have the Europeans achieved continental stability for the price of their loss of democratic control over EU institutions and policies? The very complexity of the decision-making processes erects a huge barrier to democratic accountability, much less citizen participation. The "political class" of Europe and of its fifteen member states may indeed share a wide range of values, policy goals, and normal political skills and behaviors, mostly forged out of the public eye through years-long apprenticeships in bargaining, negotiation, and political compromise. Unfortunately, this does not a democracy make. This is classic elite formation, more like the socialization and professional training of young lawyers, doctors, or bankers than the complex trajectories of political careers beginning in all walks of life, as is normal in a multi-party European parliamentary democracy.[18]

One is left with a deep disquiet, not about political stability or economic security in Europe, but about our ultimate ability to build full-fledged, participatory democracy under the conditions of relentless globalization. Paradoxically, it may not be globalization

---

18. There is a huge literature on democracy in Europe, much of it addressing the perceived "democratic deficit" in the European Union. In addition to works already cited, I have found the following helpful: Philippe C. Schmitter, How to Democratize the European Union and Why Bother? (Boulder, 2000); David Held, Democracy and the Global Order (Stanford, Calif., 1995); and Barry Holden, ed., Global Democracy: Key Debates (London, 2000).

per se that erodes democratic practices, though there are some who argue that is the case. It may be that it is precisely our attempts to build institutional barriers to protect us from the worst consequences of globalization that most threaten democracy in the first world, to say nothing at all about the prospects for democracy in rapidly developing parts of central Europe and the third world. This is surely the most difficult problem that the post-modern state must address.

Aristotelian Political Science: *Bildungspolitik* and the End of Sovereignty

James Bernard Murphy

In the Aristotelian tradition, the sovereign[1] (that is, plenary) authority of the state rests upon its claim to be a complete community (*autarkeia* or *perfecta*), that is, to provide its citizens with a setting sufficiently large and complex to make possible full human flourishing. According to Aristotelian political science, then, it is not surprising that less than perfect communities, such as the family, village, or corporation lack plenary authority, for they are not large or complex enough to afford the full range of opportunities for human flourishing. We permit these imperfect communities to exercise authority in proportion to their capacity to promote human flourishing; thus parents, for example, have wider and more comprehensive authority than employers, because

---

I am indebted to the Earhart Foundation and to the Pew Charitable Trusts for their financial support during the research and writing of this chapter. I am also indebted to the comments of Marcus Fischer, Roger Masters, Ian Lustick, Ted Miller, David Peritz, Mark Murphy, Robert Audi, and Ronald Beiner on an earlier draft. Finally I wish to thank the participants of the conference "Rethinking the State," held in Berlin, September 21-23, 2000, for their invaluable criticisms and suggestions.

1. By "sovereign" I do not refer to Augustinian sovereignty but to Aristotle's notion of plenary political authority, that is, authority to regulate the whole range of human activity by means of the full range of legal powers, including powers to banish and to execute.

parents play a much more important role in the development of human person than employers. In Aristotelian political science, the degree and range of authority permitted in a community must be calibrated to the capacity of that community to promote human flourishing. We do not permit these imperfect communities the powers over life, liberty, and property granted exclusively to the political community.

In modern political theory, the state is usually identified with more modest aspirations, such as the rule of law (*Rechtsstaat*), a monopoly on the legitimate uses of violence, and the management of the domestic political economy. For Aristotle, however, the end of the state could not be identified with law, order, or wealth because he understood these values to be merely instruments to human flourishing and happiness. As instruments, they must be limited by the end they serve, meaning that for Aristotle a state could have too much law, too much order, and too much wealth. Even the noblest aspirations of the modern state, liberty and equality, are not, for Aristotle, ultimate ends. He is neither a libertarian nor an egalitarian. According to him, the demands of liberty and equality must be subordinated to the demands of justice, and justice is understood as the legal and institutional arrangements that promote the common good of the political community – a common good inseparable from the flourishing of each of its members. Aristotle's insistence that the state must be oriented to the full actualization of the capacities of its citizens has led many modern commentators to observe that the Aristotelian state resembles a modern church or university more than a modern government.

I propose to explore the meaning of this Aristotelian political science and his understanding of *Bildungspolitik* in the *Bildungsstaat*. At the end, I will consider how the growth of international commerce, society, law and government might affect the claims of the modern nation-state to sovereign or plenary authority. I will pose this question: if the modern state must relinquish its claim to be a perfect community, then must not it also relinquish its claim to sovereign authority?

The best and most illuminating approach to Aristotelian political science would be an actual empirical investigation of politics oriented to a pressing normative concern — for example, a study of the effects of economic polarization on democratic participation. Such an Aristotelian political science would be at once empirical and ethical — in stark contrast to both our contemporary philosophical ethics, which generally lacks a concern for the empirical context of moral excellence, and our contemporary social sciences, which either lack a normative dimension altogether or degrade practical reason into an instrument for the satisfaction of desire ("rational choice"). Presumably an Aristotelian political science would reject both our apolitical ethics and our amoral political science; it would combine a rich empirical analysis of how the concrete circumstances of choice shape the capacities of individuals to variously realize or ruin the genuine goods of human fulfillment. Such a political science would attempt to interpret and explain individual ethical choices in their political contexts: how does our democratic regime, for example, shape our marriages and our families, our ways of teaching and worshiping? Or, more generally, how do our political and economic institutions promote or frustrate excellence of practical deliberation among our citizens? At the same time, Aristotelian political science would attempt to interpret and explain the political choices of communities in terms of the ethical character of their members: Does our political reluctance to send troops abroad reflect a lack of martial virtue among our citizens or a healthy popular skepticism about foreign adventures? Do political proposals for tax-cuts reflect widespread greed among our citizens or prudent doubts about the wisdom of government spending? Or, given the reluctance of our citizens to sacrifice a measure of individual liberty for the common good, do proposals for universal mandatory national service make sense?

In lieu of such an actual study, I will merely identify some of the conceptual elements of an Aristotelian political science and how they might be related to each other. There are, I think, two main pillars to the conceptual architecture of such a science: first, the notion that political science must be architectonic, meaning that it must range over the variety of kinds of order found in social and political life and, hence, over the range of sciences that study those kinds of order; and second, the notion that political science is practical, meaning that its investigations must be oriented toward illuminating the deliberations of citizens (especially statesmen). As we shall see, in Aristotelian political science these two pillars are not free-standing but closely connected such that the principles of explanatory science are simultaneously the principles of moral excellence. Finally, to explore "Aristotelian" political science, I will sometimes compare the views of Aristotle and of Thomas Aquinas on these topics; Aristotle and Aquinas agree enough to make a comparison possible, yet they differ enough to make the comparison illuminating. I will offer my own critical appraisal of that comparison as well as engage in some broadly Aristotelian reflections on political science.

1. Political Science as Architectonic: The Kinds of Human Order.

Thomas Aquinas learned from Augustine rather than from Aristotle to treat order as the object of scientific inquiry. As he says in the prologue to his commentary on the *Nicomachean Ethics*: "to be wise is to establish order. The reason for this is that wisdom is the most powerful perfection of reason, whose characteristic is to know order."[2] Order, in the sense of a pattern, system, or structure, provides a basis for descriptive and explanatory inference. Order, as F. A. Hayek puts it, is "a state of affairs in which a multiplicity of elements of various kinds are so related to each other that we may learn from our acquaintance with some spatial or temporal part of the whole to form correct expectations concerning the rest, or at least expectations which have a good chance of proving correct."[3] This broadly philosophical conception of order contrasts sharply with the narrowly ideological conception of order in mainstream social science, where order in the sense of social stability or peace between nations is usually assumed without argument to be the goal of all scientifically-informed public policy. We might contrast the philosophical and the ideological senses of order by observing that there are kinds of order that are not in the least orderly.

In the Aristotelian tradition, the kinds of sciences of human affairs[4] are grounded in the kinds of order in human affairs; thus,

---

2. S. Thomae Aquinatis Opera Omnia, ed. Robertus Busa SI (Stuttgart, 1980), vol. 4 Sententia Libri Ethicorum (Prologue, n.1). All translations from the Latin are mine.

3. F. A. Hayek, Law, Legislation, and Liberty, vol. 1 (Chicago, 1973), p. 36. Hayek here draws on Stebbing: "When we know how a set of elements is ordered we have a basis for inference." L. S. Stebbing, A Modern Introduction to Logic (London, 1950), p. 228. It is surprising that Hayek, a leading modern theorist of order, should nowhere, to my knowledge, cite the seminal contribution of Thomas Aquinas.

4. Aristotle's pluralistic conception of the human sciences is evident when he says that, in addition to ethics, we need to consider legislative science and constitutional law "to complete the philosophy of human affairs (peri ta

the adequacy of an account of the diverse kinds of human sciences depends upon the adequacy of the prior account of the diverse kinds of order. In the first part of this chapter I will outline an account of the kinds of social order — an account rooted in Aristotle and developed by the Spanish Jesuits of the sixteenth century, the economists of the Scottish Enlightenment, and their heirs.[5] I will then attempt to show the superiority of this broadly Aristotelian account of social order both to the prior Sophistic accounts and to the subsequent Thomistic account. In the second part of the chapter, I will argue that because Aristotle roots the order of deliberate human action in the order of nature and the order of custom, he enables us to see not only the proper relation of political science to ethics but also the proper relation of explanation to interpretation in political science.[6] In the final part, I consider the ways in which political science is and ought to be practical.[7]

---

    anthrōpeia philosophia)." See Nicomachean Ethics 1181b 15. Bekker numbers from Greek text edited by L. Bywater (Oxford, 1894).

5. In the analysis of Aristotle's account of the three kinds of order, I draw freely on my book, The Moral Economy of Labor: Aristotelian Themes in Economic Theory (New Haven, 1993), chaps. 2 and 4.

6. Here I follow the lead of Stephen G. Salkever who has long and rightly argued that Aristotelian social science cannot be reduced to either the explanatory or the interpretive; see his "Aristotle's Social Science" in Essays on the Foundations of Aristotelian Political Science, ed. Carnes Lord and David K. O'Connor (Berkeley, 1991), pp. 11-48.

7. Throughout this chapter I interpret Aristotle according to a procedure of philosophical reconstruction, which combines literal exegesis with a more creative exploration of his thought in the contexts of the Aristotelian tradition (chiefly Thomas Aquinas) and of contemporary debates in social theory. See the discussion of the method of "reconstruction" in Fred D. Miller's Nature, Justice, and Rights in Aristotle's *Politics* (Oxford, 1995), pp. 21-22.

In Book VII of Aristotle's *Politics* we find this cryptic passage: "In order to become good and wise (*agathos kai spoudaios*) requires three things; these are nature, habit, and reason (*physis, ethos, logos*)"[8] Few sentences in the Aristotelian corpus, I think, are as richly suggestive as is this one — or as much in need of both interpretation and imaginative reconstruction. Obviously each of these terms, nature, habit, reason, is at the center of Aristotle's conceptual vocabulary; what is less obvious is that this ordered triad is echoed throughout his writings. From the immediate context we can see that Aristotle is speaking in the first place of the components of moral and intellectual self-realization: we must begin with the right natural powers and dispositions, we must cultivate these powers and dispositions into the right habits of character, and we must use reason to reflectively adjust our habits in light of our stipulated moral ideals. In this model of human self-realization, our habits presuppose human nature but cannot be reduced to it, just as our stipulated rational ideals presuppose our habits but cannot be reduced to them.

Aristotle extended his triad beyond individual self-realization to the actualization of the political community. Thus, he says in many places, the legislator, in the deliberate stipulations of law (*nomos*), must take into account the natural capacities of his citizens as well as their social customs (*ethé* or *agraphoi nomoi*). In the subsequent Aristotelian tradition we find this triad employed in the analysis of several other social institutions. In jurisprudence we find many variants of expressions for natural, customary, and stipulated or positive law.[9] In logic we find John Poinsot (John of

---

8. Politics 1332a 38. Bekker numbers from Greek text edited by W. D. Ross (Oxford, 1957). All translations from the Greek are mine.
9. Thus the author of the Rhetorica Ad Herennium (II, 19) lists the departments of ius as: "natura, lege, consuetudine, indicato, aequo et bono, pacto." Ulpian

St. Thomas) asking "whether the division of signs into natural (*naturale*), stipulated (*ad placitum*), and customary (*ex consuetudine*) is a sound division."[10] By natural signs he means those signs that relate to their objects independent of human activity: smoke is a sign of fire. By customary signs he means those signs that arise from the collective and nonreflective practices of human communities: napkins on a table are a sign that dinner is imminent. By stipulated signs he means those signs whose meaning is deliberately appointed by an individual, as when a new word is introduced. Although Poinsot does not refer to Aristotle in his discussion of the threefold division of signs, I argue that he is offering here an interpretation and extension of Aristotle's nature, custom, and reason.[11]

Finally, F.A. Hayek employs this triad, at least implicitly, in his analysis of the three kinds of order: "Yet much of what we call culture is just such a spontaneously grown order [custom], which arose neither altogether independently of human action [nature] nor by design [stipulation], but by a process that stands between these two possibilities, which were long considered as exclusive

---

famously distinguishes (Digest I, 1.1) ius naturale, ius gentium, ius civile. And Cicero (De Inventione II, 53.160) deploys the Aristotelian scheme in his famous passage on the evolution of law from principles of nature to deliberate statutes: "Law (ius) initially proceeds from nature, then certain rules of conduct become customary by reason of their advantage; later still both the principles that proceeded from nature and those that had been approved by custom received the support of religion and the fear of the law (lex)."

10. John Poinsot, Tractatus de Signis [1632], ed. and trans. John Deely (Berkeley, 1985), p. 269.

11. For a critique and reconstruction of Poinsot's doctrine of signs, see James Bernard Murphy, "Nature, Custom, and Stipulation in the Semiotic of John Poinsot," Semiotica 83 1/2 (1991), pp. 33-68.

alternatives."[12] Hayek's distinction between the spontaneous order of custom and the designed order of stipulation is drawn from Adam Ferguson: "Nations stumble upon establishments, which are indeed the result of human action, but not the execution of any human design."[13] Hayek gives pride of place, however, in the discovery of spontaneous social order to the Spanish Jesuit Luis Molina, who explained that natural price "results from the thing itself without regard to laws and decrees, but is dependent on many circumstances which alter it, such as the sentiments of men, their estimation of different uses, often even in consequence of whims and pleasures."[14] Following the lead of the theorists of order from Aquinas to Hayek, therefore, I will now reconstruct Aristotle's triad in terms of three fundamental concepts of order: there is the natural order of physical, chemical, and biological processes; there is the customary order of habitual social practices; and there is the stipulated order of deliberate design. In Aristotelian political science, the unit of analysis is an institution or practice (some stable pattern of human action or interaction) and the level of analysis is natural order, customary order, or stipulated order. Our three kinds of order form the three dimensions of every human practice or institution, meaning that explanation must involve analysis at the levels of the sciences of nature, the sciences of custom, and the sciences of rational stipulation. Thus the study of language involves the natural sciences of psychology and

---

12. F. A. Hayek, "Kinds of Order in Society" [1964], in The Politicization of Society, ed. Kenneth Templeton, Jr. (Indianapolis, 1979), p. 509.

13. Adam Ferguson, An Essay on the History of Civil Society (Edinburgh, 1767), p. 187.

14. Luis Molina, De iustitia et iure (Cologne, 1596-1600), tom. II, disp. 347, no. 3. Cited in F.A. Hayek Law, Legislation, and Liberty, vol. 1, pp. 21 and 151.

physiology, the customary sciences of linguistic drift and analogy-formation, and the rational sciences of rhetoric and logic. Each of these levels of analysis is crucial to the explanation of the complex order we find in language. We can now see that, despite his seminal contributions to the sciences of order, Hayek tended to confuse the unit of analysis with the level of analysis: he thus assigned the "market" (which is not itself a single institution but a metaphor embracing a huge range of institutions and practices) exclusively to the spontaneous order of custom.[15] Yet market practices involve all three kinds of order: natural propensities toward exchange, customs of fairness and good faith, as well as deliberate stipulations defining what can and cannot be exchanged.

How does this triad differ from the more familiar dichotomy of nature and convention? First of all, the concept of convention collapses the important distinction between the tacit social order of custom and the individually designed order of stipulation; when something is described as conventional we don't know if the claim is that it was deliberately stipulated or that it arose spontaneously. Second, ever since Antiphon set nature and convention in opposition, they have usually been treated as mutually exclusive alternatives; some Sophists championed nature while others championed convention.[16] Indeed, no set of concepts has so dominated social theory, from ancient times through the present, as the nature-convention dichotomy; one prominent contemporary social theorist, G. A. Cohen, asserts: "The Sophists'

---

15. "Such spontaneous orders we find not only in the working of institutions like language and law ... but also in the relations of the market." Hayek, "Kinds of Order in Society," p. 509.

16. Antiphon and Callicles champion physis over nomos; for Antiphon see Die Fragmente der Vorsokratiker, ed. Hermann Diels and Walter Kranz (Berlin, 1954), frag. 44A.

distinction between nature and convention is the foundation of all social criticism."[17] Yet Aristotle insists that nature, custom, and stipulation are mutually inclusive and form a nested hierarchy such that every social institution or practice has a natural, customary, and stipulated dimension. Finally, the opposition of nature and convention serves a reductive explanatory strategy: either the claim that what seems to have rich symbolic and moral meaning, for example, marriage, is really just a biological strategy for reproductive fitness; or the claim that what seems to be rooted in a strong natural impulse, for example, marriage, is really just a cultural construct. Aristotle seems to reject such reductionist strategies as when he observes in the *Nicomachean Ethics*: "Now some think that we are become good by nature (*physei*), others by habit (*ethei*), others by being taught (*didakē*)."[18] As we discover from the parallel passage in the *Politics*, Aristotle thinks that each of these views is right but also incomplete: we need nature, habits, and reason.

In accordance with Aristotle's explicit logic of classification, I have thus far treated nature, custom, and rational stipulation as three species of the genus "order." But this genus-species logic does not indicate the serial and hierarchical relations among our three concepts: nature is prior to custom and custom is prior to stipulation. Aristotle however, offers an alternative logic of classification, which is most clearly illustrated by his analysis of the kinds of souls. Here, instead of defining the genus "soul" and the species of plant, animal, and human souls, Aristotle says that the plant soul is living (that is, nutritive and reproductive), the animal soul is living plus sensitive, and the human soul is living and

---

17. G. A. Cohen, Karl Marx's Theory of History (Princeton, 1978), p. 107.

18. Nicomachean Ethics 1179b 20.

sensitive plus rational.[19]

Aristotle implicitly treats nature, custom, and stipulation as such a hierarchy: "In every case the lower faculty can exist apart from the higher, but the higher presupposes those below it."[20] Nature represents the physical, chemical, and biological processes of the cosmos; nature can and did exist apart from human custom and stipulation. Human custom is rooted in the physiology of habit but transcends habit by becoming a social system of norms. Custom presupposes nature, but custom can exist without being the object of rational reflection and stipulation: language existed before grammarians. Stipulation is the synoptic order deliberately imposed upon the pre-reflective materials of custom; reflective stipulation always presupposes custom. We have thus far treated "nature" as the causal properties that are actualized by custom and stipulation; but does not Aristotle also describe the full-blown actualization of a thing's potential as natural?[21] A full discussion of Aristotle's many senses of "nature" would be out of place here, but I will only observe that Aristotle does sometimes distinguish what is "by nature" (*physei*) from what is "according to nature" (*kata physin*).[22] What is broadly "by nature" might be either according to nature (if it realizes its end) or contrary to nature (*para physin*, if it does not). Thus fire is "by nature" whether the flame goes up (according to nature) or is blown down (contrary to nature); birth

---

19. De Anima (414a 29 — 415a 13).

20. R. D. Hicks, Aristotle: De Anima (Cambridge, 1907), p. 335.

21. Ronald Beiner brought this passage to my attention (Politics 1252b 32): "nature is an end: what each thing is — for example, a human being, a horse, or a household — when its coming into being is complete is, we assert, the nature of that thing."

22. See, for one example, Physics 193a 1-2.

is "by nature" whether of a normal baby (according to nature) or of a deformed baby (contrary to nature). Nature, as employed in his progressive hierarchy, corresponds most closely to Aristotle's concept of natural potential (*dynamis physei*).[23] By examining our triad in a variety of contexts, we will see that this progressive hierarchy is pervasive in Aristotle's thought. First, for Aristotle, nature, custom, and stipulation articulate the hierarchy of the *scala naturae*: "The other animals for the most part live by nature (*physis*), though in some respects by habit (*ethos*) as well, while man lives also by reason (*logos*), for he alone has reason."[24] One fascinating aspect of this comment is that *ethos*, habit or custom, is the bridge between animals and man; thus, as we shall later see, the sciences of custom must mix explanation and interpretation.

Second, nature, custom, and stipulation form the same progressive hierarchy in individual development as they do in the scale of nature: ontogeny recapitulates phylogeny. Aristotle says that there are three kinds of human faculties (*dynameis*): those that are innate (*suggenēs*), those that come by practice (*ethos*), and those that come from teaching (*mathēsis*).[25] These three faculties form a hierarchy: "The contribution of nature clearly does not depend on us . . . while argument (*logos*) and teaching (*didakē*) surely do not influence everyone, but the soul of the student must have been prepared by habit (*ethos*)."[26] Our nature, he says, is given at birth while our natural potentials are trained by habit;

---

23. See Physics 193a 1 and Generations of Animals 770b 9 and 767b 5. For a fuller discussion of the distinction between physei and kata physin, see my Moral Economy of Labor, pp. 124-129.

24. Politics, 1332b 2.

25. Metaphysics 1047b 31.

26. Nicomachean Ethics 1179b 21.

teaching invites us to reflect on our habits and perhaps stipulate new ones.

Third, this hierarchy plays a parallel role in the political development of a community as it does in the moral development of an individual. The first task of a legislator, says Aristotle, is to regulate the biological nature of the citizens through eugenics (*eugeneia* or *aretē genous*); his second task is to instill the proper habits in each citizen through and educational regime aimed at developing the right political disposition (*euhexia politikē*); his final task is to reflect on his first two tasks by studying political science.[27] "We have already considered what natures are likely to be most easily molded by the hands of the legislator. All else is the work of education; we learn some things by habit and other things by being taught."[28] Just as the legislator is responsible for attempting to shape the natural potentials and the tacit customs of his city, so every mature person is responsible for making the best he can of his natural potentials and his habits of character. Yet neither the legislator nor any individual person has complete rational control over either social customs or moral habits.

The student of Thomas Aquinas who completed his commentary on the *Politics* of Aristotle certainly understood the hierarchical structure of Aristotle's three concepts of order: "There ought to be harmony among them, namely, nature, custom, and reason: for always the latter presupposes the former."[29] And in his

---

27. See Politics 1334b 30ff and 1336a 4.

28. Politics 1332b 8. "Now in men reason and mind are the goal of nature, so that the birth and training in custom of the citizens ought to be ordered with a view to them." Politics 1334b 15.

29. The commentary on Politics 1332 a 38 reads: "Quare hoc oportet consonare inter se, scilicet naturam, consuetudinem, et rationem: semper enim posterius

commentary on the *Nicomachean Ethics*, Aquinas analyzes the mutually complementary roles of nature, habit, and doctrine in the moral development of an individual.[30] Yet in his formal account (in the prologue to his commentary on the *Ethics*) of the kinds of order Aquinas does not refer to the Aristotelian hierarchy. He says that there are four kinds of order: the first is the order that reason does not make but only beholds, the order of nature; the second is the order that reason makes in its own acts, as when it arranges concepts and signs of concepts; the third is the order that reason makes in the operations of the will; the fourth is the order that reason makes in the external things it produces.[31]

In terms of our Aristotelian triad, Aquinas's four orders actually reduce to two: order independent of human action (namely, the order of nature) and order made by deliberate human action (namely the order stipulated by reason in thought, deeds, and artifacts). There seems to be nothing corresponding to the order of custom, an order that is the product of human action but never wholly the execution of any design. Yet this kind of order — an order powerfully illustrated in natural language, in common law, in market exchange — is precisely the order that is the primary object of inquiry in social theory. Here Aquinas, following Aristotle, tends to assimilate custom either to nature, as "second nature" or to rational stipulation, as "unwritten law."[32] But such

---

praesupponit prius." In: In Libros Politicorum Aristotelis Expositio, ed. Raymundi Spiazzi (Turin, 1951), p. 386.

30. See Aquinas, In Decem Libros Ethicorum Aristotelis Ad Nicomachum Expositio, ed. Raymundi Spiazzi (Turin, 1949), Lib. VII, lec. 10, l.14 [2143 ff].

31. Sententia Libri Ethicorum (Prologue, n.1).

32. For many examples of how Aristotle tends to reduce custom to either nature or law see my Moral Economy of Labor, chap. 4.

attempts to reduce custom either to nature or to law obscure what is distinctive about customary order. For, as Hayek and others have shown, the complexity of the evolving order exhibited in language, markets, and law surpasses the stipulative capacities of any person or persons — even if aided by supercomputers. That the order found in these core institutions of social life cannot be understood merely as the product of deliberate human reason is clear when we reflect upon the unpredictable pattern of their evolution: because of the complex path-dependence of the evolution of custom, the sciences of customary order tend to be historical and retrospective rather than deductive and predictive. When one considers that every utterance made by a speaker of English shapes the language, that every purchase shapes the market price, that every act of litigation, adjudication, and legislation shapes the law, we begin to appreciate the complexity of social order. By contrast to this kind of social order, Aquinas focuses in the prologue on the order found in an army, as does John Finnis in his exposition of Aquinas.[33] But the deliberately stipulated order of battle is a very misleading exemplar of the complex and evolutionary order found in core social institutions. Indeed, the attempt by several modern societies to reorder language, law, and the market on the model of military command shows how dangerous it is to confuse the spontaneous order of custom with the order of deliberate stipulation.

Although Aquinas explicitly distinguishes the order found in action from the order found in production on the grounds that action (*actio*) is perfective of the agent while production (*factio*) is perfective of the artifact[34], he nonetheless frequently compares the

---

33. Aquinas, Sententia Libri Ethicorum (Prologue, n.5); John Finnis, Aquinas: Moral Political, and Legal Theory (Oxford, 1998), pp. 32-35.

34. Aquinas, Sententia Libri Ethicorum, Prologue, n. 13.

stipulated order found in human actions to the stipulated order of found in artifacts: "When, however, human reason has to order not only the things that are used by men but also men themselves, who are ruled by reason, it proceeds in either case from the simple to the complex: in the case of the things used by man when, for example, it builds a ship out of wood and a house out of wood and stones; in the case of men themselves when, for example, it orders many men so as to form a certain society."[35] And rather than contrast the order reason discovers in custom from the order reason makes in stipulation, Aquinas describes both social and political order as something reason brings about: "the state is a certain whole that human reason not only knows but also brings about (*cognoscitiva et operativa*)."[36]

2. Political Science as Architectonic: The Kinds of Human Sciences

2.1 A Range of Kinds of Order Means a Range of Kinds of Sciences of Politics

Aristotle does not explicitly link the diversity of sciences to the diversity of his three kinds of order. True, he does distinguish theoretical from practical sciences on the ground that the objects of theoretical science do not change while the objects of practical science do change; this difference means both that the objects of theoretical science are of a higher dignity than the objects of

---

35. Aquinas, Sententia Libri Politicorum, Prologue, n. 4.
36. Aquinas, Sententia Libri Politicorum, Prologue, n. 6.

practical science and that the theoretical sciences admit of greater precision than do the practical sciences.[37] Aquinas more precisely links diversity of kinds of order to diversity of sciences: to the order that reason beholds but does not make (which Aquinas limits to nature) belongs natural philosophy; to the order that reason makes in its own acts, belongs what he calls "rational philosophy" or logic; to the order that reason makes in the operations of the will belongs moral philosophy; and to the order that reason makes in external things belong the mechanical arts.[38]

Yet, as we shall see, the Aristotelian account of the kinds of order in human society will enable us to develop a more adequate understanding of the kinds of human sciences than will the Thomistic account. By defining the order of human affairs rather narrowly as "those that proceed from the will of man according to the order of reason," Aquinas must exclude from social and political theory (what he calls "moral philosophy") all those dimensions of human practice not directly subject to deliberate will: the equilibrium of markets, evolution of language and of law, the whole realm of tacit prejudices, values, beliefs, and practices. He says that "if some operations are found in man that are not subject to the will and reason, they are not properly called human but natural . . . ."[39] Yet, as we shall see, natural science alone is not adequate to the study of the order of custom; the order of custom requires human sciences, both explanatory and interpretive. Now one might defend Aquinas by supposing that his moral philosophy, rooted in the study of intentional human acts, provides him with the capacity to judge the morality of choices

---

37. Aristotle, Metaphysics 1025b 19-27 and 1065b 1-5.
38. Aquinas, Sententia Libri Ethicorum Prologue, n. 2.
39. Aquinas, Sententia Libri Ethicorum Prologue, n. 3.

with respect to markets, language, law, and prejudice; perhaps the agent doesn't need to understand these phenomena in order to act properly with respect to them. But Aquinas's strong emphasis on prudence in moral choice, on the capacity to understand the implications of one's acts, not only on oneself, but on others as well, shows us that understanding the customary dimension of institutions will be of great moral urgency to citizens and especially to legislators. Thus Aquinas insists that a legislator may have to tolerate various moral vices and usurious lending practices, that a judge may have to enforce unjust laws, if, in his judgment, the disturbance of the customary order is too great.[40] But to make this judgment, or at least to make it well, depends upon one's understanding of systems of exchange and of prejudice well enough to roughly estimate the impact of deliberate interventions in these spontaneous orders. Aquinas is aware, in a very general way, of the danger that deliberate interventions in customary processes can have perverse effects; but he has no adequate grasp of the order of custom or of the sciences that might illuminate that order.

2.2 Ethics as a Branch of Political Science

Aristotle's subordination of the study of ethics to the study of politics strikes us as odd. He opens his *Nicomachean Ethics* by arguing that the study of ethics must be ordered to the comprehensive science of human good, namely, political science; and he ends his *Ethics* by insisting that the study of ethics culminates in the science of legislation. Moreover, he repeatedly

---

40. See Aquinas, Summa Theologiae, IaIIae, 96.2c, 96.4c; IIaIIae, 78.1 ad 3.

refers to the subject matter of his *Nicomachean Ethics* as a "political inquiry."[41] What are we to make of this politicized ethics? I think we can best grasp the essential power and insight of Aristotle's understanding of the political nature of ethics by contrasting it with Aquinas's more modern notion of an autonomous science of ethics.

Moral philosophy, at least as Aquinas understands it in these prologues,[42] is relatively autonomous from political science because the unit of analysis is human acts rather than human persons. As we shall see, his focus on human acts deflects attention from the psychological, social, and political context of those acts. He opens the second, and by far the longest, part of the *Summa* by saying: "Man is said to be made in the image of God, according to which is signified that he is intelligent, master of himself, and with free judgment; now since we have agreed that God is the exemplar cause of things and that they issue from His power through his will, it remains to consider his image, that is to say, man as the source of his own deeds, having free judgment and power over his deeds."[43] This passage, and many others that follow, link self-

---

41. See NE 1094b 11 and 1095b 5-6; for a very different view of the political dimension of the Nicomachean Ethics see Richard Bodéüs, The Political Dimensions of Aristotle's *Ethics*, trans. Jan Edward Garrett (Albany, 1993).

42. These are the Prologues to the commentary on the ethics, to the commentary on the politics, and to the Prima Secundae of the Summa. One could, no doubt, interpret Aquinas's account of the virtues in the Secunda Secundae, as an effort to understand human actions in the psychological and social contexts in which virtues and vices are acquired. I do not deny that there are resources within Aquinas's philosophy to understand ethics in a more political context.

43. Aquinas, Summa Theologiae, Prologue to IaIIae. Aquinas's explicit reliance on the theological premise of the *imago Dei* as the basis for his assertion of human free choice raises the question of to what extent the doctrine of free choice depends upon revealed truths. Finnis, who omits all reference to the

mastery with freedom of judgment between alternative courses of action in rational deliberation: a person is master of his actions (*dominus suorum actuum*) inasmuch as he has free decision (*liberum arbitrium*) through his faculties of will and reason: "Therefore a person is master of his acts through reason and will: whence his free decision is called a faculty of reason and will. Therefore those acts alone are properly called human which proceed from his own deliberate willing."[44] As John Finnis formulates Aquinas's teaching here: "One has this mastery or dominion (*dominium*) over one's own actions precisely in that one's will is not forced to one or another of opposing proposals."[45]

Yet this alleged link between free choice and self-mastery turns out to be largely illusory because the freedom of a person's choices tells us little about whether that person is free. As MacIver rightly observes: "What is free, however, is the choice between alternatives not the choice of what the alternatives shall be."[46] A slave may well exercise free choice among all the genuine alternatives of choice before him; but those alternatives are so radically impoverished that his self-mastery, his freedom for self-determination is a chimera. Why is this so? Because I cannot deliberate about potential courses of action unless I believe that

---

imago Dei in his discussion of this passage, seems to deny the necessity of a theological premise (see his Aquinas, p. 20); Germain Grisez, by contrast, argues that "only believers accept the reality of free choice" (see his Christian Moral Principles [Chicago, 1983], p. 67).

44. Aquinas, Summa Theologiae IaIIae, 1.1c.

45. Finnis, Aquinas, p. 20n 3.

46. R. M. MacIver, Social Causation (New York, 1942), p. 241.

each alternative can be realized by my conduct.[47] To will something is not merely to wish for it. Thus, the range of our deliberations, the range of the alternatives of action before us, depends upon many physical, biological, psychological, social, and political conditions beyond our direct control. Some of these conditions are natural necessities that must be accepted as merely a given in practical deliberation; they cannot be meaningfully said to constrain our freedom and self-mastery because these concepts assume the human condition. But the most profound, far-reaching, and morally troubling constraints on the capacity for individual self-determination can only be addressed by psychological, social, and political theory; indeed, addressing those unnecessary constraints on the capacity for full self-realization must be the main agenda of those sciences.

John Finnis insists that, according to Aquinas, "to deny that human persons are each masters of their own acts is to assert something 'impossible, and destructive of all moral philosophy and socio-political life."[48] This astonishing statement is true only if free choice among given alternatives is sufficient for self-mastery; but, as we have argued, real self-mastery and real freedom depends upon the degree of control we have over the alternatives of choice. To see why substantial control over the agenda of deliberation is crucial for self-determination we can consider the experience of

---

47. Aquinas follows Aristotle in distinguishing choice from mere wish and in arguing that no one chooses save what he thinks he can do himself: impossibilities cannot be objects of choice. See Aristotle, Nicomachean Ethics 1111b 20-25 and Aquinas Summa Theologiae, IaIIae, 13.4c, 13.5c, 14.4c. But, as Robert Audi reminded me, perhaps I can deliberately choose to do what is in fact impossible so long as I believe it is possible.

48. Finnis, Aquinas, p. 20n 3, quoting from the Summa Contra Gentiles II c.60 n. 5.

many political communities over time that have exercised "democratic" and "free" deliberation without control over the political agenda, which is set by a foreign power or ruling clique. Without substantial control over the agenda of political deliberation, that deliberation, however free, is a mockery of true self-determination; such a dependent political community is in the position of our slave.[49]

What this means is that politics, broadly understood, does not just provide a set of constraints and opportunities external to ethical deliberation; rather, politics, in the sense of the whole social context of action, is internal to the very act of ethical deliberation and choice. I can choose only what I think I can achieve by my efforts; and politics determines the range of what a given person can expect to achieve and so the range of his choice. We do not formulate our individual ethical ends and then look to see if they are feasible in a given political (including social and economic) context; rather, our understanding of political feasibility shapes our very capacity to formulate our ends.

Aristotle does not describe acts as being done freely or not[50] but he does describe persons as free or not; more precisely, he describes persons as having degrees of freedom: a citizen has more freedom than a mere subject, a democratic citizen has more freedom than an oligarchic citizen, a master has more freedom than a slave, a master-craftsman more than a wage-laborer, a man more than a woman, an adult more than a child, and an educated person more than an ignorant person. And where Aquinas posits freedom and self-mastery as axioms, Aristotle sees them as goals subject to

---

49. On the importance of control over the agenda of deliberation for democratic politics, see Robert Dahl, Democracy and Its Critics (New Haven, 1989), pp. 112-114.

50. Aristotle considers whether acts are voluntary, not whether they are free.

varying degrees of achievement; as we shall see, Aristotle's approach invites empirical investigation of the conditions that enhance or diminish freedom of persons.

Aristotle's conception of the freedom (*eleutheria*) of persons is complex: I will only attempt to outline some of its elements. Like many concepts, "freedom" gets much of its meaning by its implied contrast terms; and Aristotle's notion of freedom embodies a number of distinct contrasts. To begin with, a free person differs from a slave, in that a free person exists for himself and not for another; a free man does not live at the beck and call of another.[51] Thus, at a minimum, a free person is not subject to the arbitrary will of another person. Yet Aristotle insists that not only slaves, but also mechanics (*banausoi*) and laborers (*thētes*) are not truly free: the menial worker is a wage slave.[52] Workers are servile, not because they are subject to the arbitrary will of another person (they are subject to the citizen class, not to individual masters) but because they are utterly subject to necessity. Yet the free activities that make for free men and for free cities begin where necessities are already in place; free men and free cities require leisure. Aristotle even says that human beings did not pursue philosophy until they had attained a comfortable standard of living.[53] So we are free only insofar as we can concern ourselves with activities beyond physical survival or even comfort.

In short, one is free to the extent that one is subject neither to the will of another nor to necessity; does this mean that freedom is living as one pleases? No: just as leisure is not merely the absence of needful occupation, but the deliberate cultivation of

---

51. Aristotle, Metaphysics 982b 25; Rhetoric 1367a 33.
52. Aristotle, Politics 1260b 1.
53. Aristotle, Metaphysics 982b 22-28.

one's moral and intellectual virtues, so freedom is not mere absence of constraint, but the rational ordering of one's passions and actions. Freedom is "living as one pleases" only for those who have achieved virtuous self-discipline; for those who have not, "living as one pleases" is a kind of slavery to mere whim.[54] Indeed, Aristotle rather paradoxically observes that in a household, the freemen are least at liberty to live as they please, while the slaves and the beasts are most at liberty to do so.[55] Freedom, thus, is not a given in the human condition, but is the highest achievement of rational discipline. The realization of freedom is precisely the aim of what is called a "liberal" education. Our education for freedom begins with our submission to the rule of law: because true freedom means the rational ordering of passions and actions, living under the law is not slavery, since law is pure reason.[56] But law can only take us so far in rational discipline; we also need the cultivation of the "liberal" arts, which is why Aristotle so often associates education with freedom and ignorance with servility.[57]

Thus, for Aristotle, the realization of free rational agency is possible only through prior submission to the authority of our parents, our teachers, and our legislators; these authorities play a crucial role in the cultivation of our passions so that they collaborate with reason in the exercise of virtue. In this developmental model of human self-realization, freedom is the fruit of obedience, and liberal independence the fruit of illiberal discipline. Freedom is emancipation through education. No doubt Aristotle's own politics was more concerned with emancipating

---

54. Aristotle, Politics, 1310a 31-35.

55. Aristotle, Metaphysics 1075a 19-23.

56. Aristotle, Politics 1310a 34-35; 1287a 28-32.

57. Aristotle, Politics 1342a 19-21 and 1338a 32.

well-born citizens from a servile warrior or commercial ethos than it was concerned with emancipating mechanics, women, and slaves from the arbitrary limits on their self-mastery.

We are now in a position to consider more precisely the relation between politics and ethics, political science and ethical science. Aristotle famously, though cryptically, says that "political science (*politikē*) and practical reason (*phronēsis*) are the same state, though to be them is not the same."[58] Politics and ethics are both about practical deliberation in the choice of what is most worthy in every occasion of choice; political science and ethical science are inquiries into the conditions, essential features, and consequences of such choices for the flourishing of individuals and communities. An individual acts ethically when he deliberates about what choices promote the best way of life as a whole for himself; an individual acts politically when he deliberates about how the community can create an environment that best promotes ethical deliberation among its members. In the final section of this chapter I will defend this claim that politics is centrally concerned with the excellence of the practical deliberation of citizens; here I will simply explore the relation between ethical and political deliberation.

Ethics and politics are obviously intimately related in the Aristotelian tradition but they have distinct foci: ethics is focused on the free choices; politics is focused on free persons and free communities. Ethical deliberation must generally take the alternatives of choice as a given; decisions often must be made now and cannot wait until new alternatives appear; moreover, individuals alone rarely have the time or power to discern substantially new alternatives of choice. Where decisions must be made soon, poli-

---

58. Nicomachean Ethics 1141b 23.

tical deliberation also must take the alternatives of choice for a community as a given; but the political community has vastly more power than does an individual to expand the alternatives of choice both for itself and for its members. Thus the distinctive focus of political deliberation is about expanding the freedom and self-mastery of persons and of communities by expanding the alternatives of choice. The foci of ethics and of politics must be kept in view as related but distinct. Too much emphasis on the ethical act of choice abstracts from the concrete conditions of choice and can lead to a kind of moral and political complacency in which free choices are taken to mean free persons. And too much emphasis on the political conditions of choice neglects the inelim- inable capacity of human beings to transcend their circumstances through free choice and can lead to a reductive determinism of ethical choice to its context. We need to understand choices in the context of the range of alternatives available in the personal and political circumstances; and we need to understand that range of alternatives (and how to expand it) in relation to the genuine freedom of choice.

Aristotle, with his rich empirical inquiry into the conditions, personal, familial, and political, that make for free persons and communities, provides better guidance than does Aquinas to the distinct focus of political science. Yet one may wonder if Aristotle does not sometimes neglect the ethical capacity of individuals on occasion to transcend their circumstances and even the settled dispositions of their characters. The first task of the legislator is to create the institutions that will inculcate the right habits in young people; failure to acquire the right habits in youth seems to make moral maturity impossible for Aristotle.[59] What would Aristotle

---

59. On legislative art, see Nicomachean Ethics 1103b 3ff; on right habituation in youth as being all important, see Nicomachean Ethics 1103b 24.

make of those (admittedly rare) instances when a mature adult manages, perhaps through Alcoholics Anonymous, against all empirical probabilities, to deliberately escape the destiny of his character? MacIntyre is probably right in answering: "the story of the thief on the cross is unintelligible in Aristotelian terms."[60] Yet we all know of persons who do manage to transcend the destiny of their bleak circumstances and even of their bad characters to choose the good.

Aquinas, by contrast, has virtually no interest in the empirical social and political context of free choices. From his vast writings we learn almost nothing about the political institutions and controversies of his day[61]; and it is revealing that he chose not to complete his commentary on the *Politics* of Aristotle. By treating free choice and self-mastery as theological axioms, Aquinas tends to neglect the political conditions of freedom for individuals and for states. Yet Aquinas's analysis of the complex interplay of reason and will in the stages of ethical deliberation goes far beyond Aristotle and is of unparalleled nuance. And Aquinas never loses sight of man's ineliminable freedom in ethical choice.

2.3 Sciences of Politics as Explanatory and Normative

Nothing is more distinctive of Aristotelian political science than the fact that nature, custom, and reason represent at once principles of theoretical explanation and principles of practical reason. He discovers the kinds of order in human affairs by asking

---

60. Alasdair MacIntyre, After Virtue (Notre Dame, Ind., 1984), p. 175.

61. On Aquinas's curious silence about the politics of his epoch, see Finnis, Aquinas, p. 3.

the question: how does one become good and excellent? Aristotle devotes considerable attention to the natural, customary, and stipulated conditions of human self-realization for goodness — whether of individuals or of states. Nature, custom, and stipulation provide either resources for or obstacles to the quest of an individual or a state to realize self-determination for goodness. Because of the diversity of the kinds of order in human affairs, all the empirical as well as the interpretive sciences will be necessary for the evaluation of the conditions for the exercise of proper freedom of self-realization. Let us begin with the natural conditions for human flourishing. In one place Aristotle says that we have no control over nature's role, which is merely the result of divine fortune or misfortune; yet in another place, he says that nature offers many potentials for good or ill that must be actualized by habits.[62] For Aristotle, medicine plays a key role in aiding individuals to overcome the natural obstacles to happiness. Medical science helps us to discern which inherited, congenital, or acquired disabilities and diseases must be treated if individuals are to real their full moral and intellectual potential; Aristotle explicitly tells us (in the *Nicomachean Ethics!*) that individuals are best cared for by a doctor with scientific knowledge of medicine.[63] In what sense is medicine a matter of practical philosophy? Consider the practical deliberations of a person with a physical or mental disability. Unless his mental disabilities or diseases are quite severe, he may well exercise full freedom of choice among the options he considers; unfortunately, however, the range of alternative courses of action that he can choose among is very likely to be significantly reduced in ways he may not even be aware of; he may make free

---

62. Nicomachean Ethics 1179b 21 and Politics 1332a 40.

63. Nicomachean Ethics 1180b 13.

choices but he is not a free person. A doctor serves a crucial moral function in the lives of his patients even if he cannot cure their disability or disease: for he can help them think more clearly about what they can or cannot do; he can partially emancipate them from a false understanding of their actual limitations. Medicine, as the science most directly responsible for understanding and shaping the natural conditions of human flourishing, must be considered a branch of political science.

But medicine alone cannot make us good people. Our natural capacities must be cultivated by the right social customs so that we acquire the right moral habits. Aristotle says: "Neither by nature, then, nor contrary to nature do the virtues arise in us; rather, we are adapted by nature to receive them, and are made perfect by habit." He also says that our rudimentary natural virtue must be transformed and perfected into habitual virtue.[64] Aristotle sees the unconscious and pre-reflective processes of the acquisition of habits and customs to be of decisive importance in the quest for moral goodness and self-mastery. A student, he says, will not even understand, let alone be persuaded by, rational moral argument unless his soul has been properly habituated to excellence.[65] Moreover, because we form our personal habits in the context of social customs, including social prejudices and ideologies, our capacity for moral self-determination is either fostered or constrained by pre-reflective patterns of thought and practice. Thus, says Aristotle, it is difficult to acquire the right moral habits if you have not been raised in a society with good customs and laws.[66]

---

64. Nicomachean Ethics 1103a 23; for natural (physikē) and true habitual (ethistē) virtue see Nicomachean Ethics, 1151a 18 and 1144b 3.
65. Nicomachean Ethics 1179b 24ff.
66. Nicomachean Ethics 1179b 32.

The main task of the legislator is to educate the citizens in virtue by habituating them to good laws and customs; and good customs may be even more important than good laws.[67]

Custom marks the bounds of reason because good custom contains the tacit conditions of reason; deliberate thought always rests upon the deeper currents of tacit and pre-reflective knowledge.[68] In Gilbert Ryle's expression, knowing that always presupposes knowing how. Only the person who knows how to cook can formulate rules of cookery; and only the person who knows how to investigate the world can formulate hypotheses.[69] We could not understand a movie or a novel if we did not already know pre-reflectively how movies and novels work — which is why we are surprised when conventions are broken. Until the experience of surprise, we were not aware of knowing the conventions. Customs provide us with the tacit expectations that simultaneously open up and close off aspects of our new experiences. As Ruth Benedict observed, it is difficult to observe our customs directly since they are the lens through which we see the world — which is why we depend upon foreigners to describe our

---

67. Nicomachean Ethics 1180a 34 and Politics 1287b 5.

68. As H.-G. Gadamer says: "We are always dominated by conventions. In every culture a series of things is taken for granted and lies fully beyond the explicit consciousness of anyone, and even in the greatest dissolution of traditional forms, mores, and customs, the degree to which things held in common still determine everyone is only more concealed." Reason in the Age of Science, trans. Frederick Lawrence (Cambridge, Mass., 1981), p. 82.

69. "In short the propositional acknowledgment of rules, reasons, or principles is not the parent of the intelligent application of them; it is a step-child of that application." Gilbert Ryle, "Knowing How and Knowing That," Proceedings of the Aristotelian Society 46 (1945-6), p. 9.

customs to us.[70] Thus, rational thought can never be wholly transparent (and self-mastery never complete) because it floats on the murky depths of tacit customary modes of thought we absorb unknowingly from the larger culture.

Custom marks the bounds of reason on the other side of rational stipulation as well: our deliberate acts reverberate through the vast networks of custom with myriad effects, intended and unintended, known and unknown, welcomed and regretted. We rarely set out to make a custom yet all of us shape custom willy-nilly every time we speak, spend money, bring forth a lawsuit, or tell a joke. By purchasing sneakers we affect the lives of workers in Indonesia for good or ill; by trying to help workers though wage-subsidies we help employers instead; by imposing liability on tobacco makers for cigarettes, we encourage efforts to impose liability on gun manufacturers for Saturday-night specials. In short, custom makes fully rational conduct impossible: we never fully know either the deeper habitual motives of our conduct or its consequences.[71]

Because custom forms the bounds of rationality, social action must be investigated, not just by the interpretation of intentions, but also by mechanisms of causal explanation. This is most obviously true in the case of the unintended consequences of actions, which by definition cannot be grasped by any interpretation of intentions or motives. We rarely intend to change the language we speak, but change it we do; and linguists require

---

70. Ruth Benedict, Patterns of Culture (1934; Boston, 1959), p. 9.

71. As Giddens puts it: "The knowledgeability of human agents, in given historical circumstances, is always bounded: by the unacknowledged conditions of action on the 'one side,' and its unintended consequences on the other." Anthony Giddens, Profiles and Critiques in Social Theory (Berkeley, 1982), p. 32.

sophisticated statistical techniques and theories of language drift to measure the unintended evolution of language. Economics is largely the science of unintended consequences of decisions to purchase, sell, invest, or save. But the tacit conditions of rational action must also be investigated empirically for the same reason that they often escape the cognizance of the agent. Thus, statistical studies have recently found that the best predictor of the imposition of the death penalty is the race of the victim — a finding that surprised many closely involved in these cases, who thought that the race of the offender would be most salient. Here the customs of racial hierarchy continue to operate behind the backs (as well as, no doubt, in the foreground) of the participants. An even more startling example was provided by another statistical study of the striking and seemingly arbitrary differences in how doctors evaluate black and white patients with the same symptoms.[72] Here the doctors involved are shocked and appalled by what has been revealed about their own actions. Myriad similar studies of the effects of race and class on professional decision-making by judges, lawyers, doctors, nurses, and others have shown that many customary biases are shaping these allegedly impartial decisions. No amount of interpretive sociology, of participant-observation, of articulating the insiders' point of view could have revealed these biases so starkly.

Of course, the empirical and the interpretive sciences must work together: often it is our interpretive insights about, for example, racial bias, that provides the hypotheses to be tested by empirical methods; or, conversely, an empirical finding that Detroit Catholics tend to vote Democratic or that Chinese women commit suicide more frequently than do Chinese men demands careful

---

72. See The New York Times, March 1, 1999, p. A21.

interpretation to give it causal significance: what precisely is it about Detroit Catholics and Chinese women that inclines them to these kinds of choices?; and these interpretations can in turn be the basis for further empirical tests. Yet whether empirical or interpretive, these sciences of human conduct are practical because they are or ought to be oriented toward enhancing the capacities for sound practical deliberation by individuals and communities. To the extent that human sciences can make me aware of some of the unacknowledged conditions of my own deliberate actions, I have a better chance of acting according to my own moral principles; to the extent that social sciences can make me aware of the possible unintended consequences of my actions, I have a better chance of acting responsibly. Aristotelian political science must have full range over all human sciences oriented toward practical deliberation.

3. Political Science as Practical: Relations to Agents

I have argued that Aristotelian political science and politics are oriented toward understanding and enhancing the conditions favoring the quest of individuals to achieve excellence through the deliberate choice of what is most worthy in every situation. But, there are beings, Aristotle reminds us, higher than human beings (the gods), activities higher than political or ethical deliberation (contemplation), and thus sciences higher than political science (theology).[73] How can political science be said to be architectonic over theoretical sciences that are superior to it? Translated into modern terms, will an architectonic Aristotelian political science

---

73. See Nicomachean Ethics 1145a 7-12. Mark Murphy brought this passage to my attention.

tend to politicize all other human activities? Theoretical activity falls under political science only in the sense that the decision to engage in theoretical activity is a matter for practical deliberation. So a sound political science, and a sound politics, will encourage citizens to pursue theoretical activity, as a supreme form of human excellence. Aristotle says that practical wisdom (ultimately, political science) issues orders for the sake of theoretical science but not to it.[74] In modern terms, politics should support and encourage the arts, sciences, and religion without attempting in any way to politicize them. Here we see a good example of the inescapably political dimension of ethical deliberation, for an individual's capacity to decide to engage in free religious, artistic, or theoretical activity will vary enormously according to the political regime.[75] In other words, an individual's choice to pursue a nonpolitical life is a deeply political question. Politics is architectonic over all other human pursuits even as it is limited by them.

Aristotelian politics is not fundamentally concerned with stabilizing social or international order, maximizing or redistributing wealth, maximizing the liberty of each as consistent with the liberty of all, or enhancing state capacity; Aristotelian politics is concerned with these goals only insofar as they can be shown to be essential for (and realized in a way compatible with) excellence of practical deliberation. But is not Aristotelian politics concerned with more than the excellence of practical deliberation among citizens? Do not Aristotle and his followers see politics as centrally concerned with human flourishing generally, with the common good, with the inculcation of the virtues, the pursuit of justice, and

---

74. Nicomachean Ethics 1145a 9.

75. Aristotle argues for the necessity of political support for apolitical leisure in Politics 1334a 4-5.

the rule of law? All this is quite true, but I shall argue that all of these concerns center on, and are unified by, the focus on the practical deliberation of citizens.

One reason that Aristotelian political science is oriented toward the choices of agents rather than to their well-being more simply is that the good on Aristotle's account is an achievement of the self and not something that can be bestowed on others. The acquisition and exercise of the moral and intellectual virtues in the enjoyment of knowledge, friendship, beauty, and political participation are not goods that can be given or distributed; they can only be enjoyed through self-actualization in the deliberate choices of individuals. As citizens, as legislators, as friends we cannot bestow the fundamental goods of human flourishing on others; at best we can help provide some resources and other opportunities, we can help remove some obstacles and constraints; but ultimately individuals must realize these goods for themselves. In short, since individual self-direction is essential to the acquisition of the virtues and the enjoyment of the deepest goods of human fulfillment, politics cannot directly bestow well-being or happiness on citizens; at best, politics can indirectly promote human flourishing by 1) liberating citizens from arbitrary constraints on the range of their practical deliberations; 2) providing citizens with the requisite instrumental means necessary for participation in the deeper goods of fulfillment; 3) encouraging the choice of the higher over the lower goods and discouraging the choice of empty or false goods.

Although Aristotle frequently speaks of politics, law, and coercion as "making" men good, as if they were clay to be molded, on a deeper level, Aristotle's own understanding of the role of deliberation in the choice of goods, his understanding of virtue as involving acting for the right reason, reveals that men cannot be "made" good, they can only be encouraged, by pressures of education and legal coercion, toward the good.[76] Good government can never entirely circumvent human choice; even our willingness to conform to the requirements of the law involves a crucial element of choice.[77] Moreover, justice and the rule of law are valuable largely because of their good effects on the deliberations of citizens. If I perceive myself as unjustly disadvantaged by a social or economic arrangement, I am much less likely voluntarily to cooperate with, or contribute to, it (who wants to be a "sucker"?); conversely, the perception of justice elicits the voluntary cooperation and contributions of citizens that are essential for the common good. And the rule of law is frequently defended on the ground that it provides a stable framework necessary for us to make plans for our future, which is why it is often more important that law be settled than it be settled right: often, our capacity for sound deliberation depends more on the stability than on the wisdom of the legal context. In short, human flourishing, the common good, the inculcation of virtue, the establishment of justice and the rule of law are all inescapably connected to, and unified by, the fundamental concern of politics for the excellence of the practical deliberation of citizens.

The resolutely practical orientation of Aristotelian political science is nowhere more manifest than in his discussions of the kinds of order; rather than catalogue the kinds of order from a theoretical or godlike point of view (as Aquinas tends to do),

---

76. On "making" men good see, for example, Nicomachean Ethics 1180b 23-5.

77. Thus Bodéüs' argument (in his The Political Dimensions of Aristotle's *Ethics*) that, according to Aristotle, only the legislator needs to understand the good because his wise legislation will "make" all others good ignores Aristotle's own awareness of the reflective dimension of virtuous actions; coercive habituation to the good may be necessary but it is not sufficient on Aristotle's account.

Aristotle's discussions always take place in the context of the practical deliberations of individuals who strive to become good and of legislators who strive to "make" men good. It is these agents who crucially need to reflect upon the natural, customary, and stipulated conditions of goodness; and it is these agents who need to reflect on where the boundary lies, in the context of their particular deliberations, between those conditions I must accept as given and those I can seek to change.

According to Aristotle, practical reason and practical philosophy have their own principles defining the goods of human flourishing and the virtues that lead us to those goods — principles that cannot be inferred from theoretical (including natural) sciences; still, practical reason and philosophy must be informed by the theoretical sciences if only because, as Leo Strauss observed, sound practical reasoning is always threatened by false theoretical views.[78] The accuracy and validity of our theoretical understanding of the world is crucial because practical and theoretical premises are so intimately intertwined in practical deliberation.

But political science is oriented toward the practical deliberations of citizens and statesmen not just as a goal but also as a starting point. For the choice of what is to be investigated (if that choice is to avoid triviality) must be guided by the concerns of agents deliberating about the good. Thus, choosing to investigate the unconscious biases that shape professional judgments makes

---

78. "The sphere governed by prudence is then in principle self-sufficient or closed. Yet prudence is always endangered by false doctrines about the whole of which man is a part by false theoretical opinions; prudence is therefore always in need of defense against such opinions, and that defense is necessarily theoretical. The theory defending prudence is misunderstood, however, if it is taken to be the basis of prudence." Leo Strauss, "Epilogue," in Essays on the Scientific Study of Politics, ed. Herbert J. Storing (New York, 1962), pp. 309-310.

sense precisely because good agents want to understand those biases in order to seek to transcend them. The political scientist is not limited to the point of view of an agent, his task is not merely to interpret and explicate that point of view; but his investigation ought to be oriented to answering questions posed by, or of concern to, an agent whom that political scientist takes to be morally good. Investigating topics either of no concern to agents or of concern only to morally bad agents will make for bad political science.[79]

But the point of view of good (or at least not wholly bad) agents varies widely and a political scientist is well advised to consider several such points of view, on the assumption that men and women of good faith, because of the diversity of the conditions of deliberation each of them faces, are likely to reason quite differently on practical questions. With his more comprehensive perspective, and deeper knowledge of the possibilities for the realization of human good, the political scientist ought to resist simply adopting the necessarily partial perspectives of the partisans in political debate. His task is to discern the insights and the blindnesses of all partisan perspectives, as Aristotle so brilliantly does in his adjudication of the conflicting views of justice advanced by the rich and poor of his day.[80] What about

---

79. Aristotle's own investigation of the methods of tyrants would seem to run afoul of this rule; yet Aristotle's explicit purpose in that investigation is to persuade a tyrant who is not wholly bad to rule more like a king. See Politics V, 11.

80. "Hence Aristotelian political science views political things in the perspective of the citizen. Since there is of necessity a variety of citizen perspectives, the political scientist or political philosopher must become the umpire, the impartial judge; his perspective encompasses the partisan perspectives because he possesses a more comprehensive and a clearer grasp of man's

fringe points of view? Are the questions raised by the radical so distant from the deliberations of ordinary citizens that they should be ignored by a political scientist? If I am a lawyer advocating greater legal protection for an oppressed group, how are the views of an anarchist, who rejects the rule of law, of any assistance in my practical deliberations? Perhaps the anarchist's perspective is so foreign to, and destructive of, legal values that it cannot offer any assistance to deliberation on the reform of legal institutions.[81] Alternatively, perhaps such a radical critique of the rule of law — and only such a radical critique — could lead ordinary lawyers to see some of the defects of legislation and adjudication and help them to design non-legal modes of regulation, coordination, and conflict-resolution.[82] All of this is just to say that Aristotelian political science, in its choice of practical points of view, must avoid the twin dangers of complacency in mainstream points of view and of irrelevance in fringe points of view.

Finally, Aristotelian political science is related to the

---

natural ends and their natural order than do the partisans." Leo Strauss, "Epilogue," p. 310.

81. Thus John Finnis criticizes the adoption of the point of view of an anarchist judge by Joseph Raz; Finnis recommends adopting as "the central case of the legal viewpoint" the point of view "in which legal obligation is treated as at least presumptively a moral obligation." See Finnis, Natural Law and Natural Rights (Oxford, 1980), pp. 13-15.

82. Thus Max Weber defends, in principle, the appointment of an anarchist law professor: "An anarchist can surely be a good legal scholar. And if he is such, then indeed the Archimedian point of his convictions, which is outside the conventions and presuppositions which are so self-evident to us, can equip him to perceive problems in the fundamental postulates of legal theory which escape those who take them for granted. Fundamental doubt is the father of wisdom." Weber, The Methodology of the Social Sciences, trans. Edward Shils and Henry Finch (New York: Free Press, 1949), p. 7.

practical deliberations of an agent in a third — and perhaps most salient — way, namely to the deliberations of someone who asks: why should I become a political scientist? This question must be at the heart of Aristotelian political science because Aristotle understands all practical inquiry and all practical conduct to be in pursuit of self-perfection. Aristotelian ethics and politics is not altruistic: according to him we do not act on behalf of others by setting aside our own good or from some abstract duty; rather, we act on behalf of others when, through love, their good becomes our own. In this sense, promoting the good of one's friends is a central mode of self-perfection for Aristotle. Yet we moderns might well want to study political science as an opportunity for altruism: to engage in the study of political things for the good of our polity and fellow citizens. Aristotle would applaud this sentiment but point out that political science has an only very indirect role to play in the promotion of political good, that often the attempt to pursue theoretical programs in practice is disastrous,[83] and that, in any event, like all would-be benefactors, political scientists are prone to greatly exaggerate the benefit they can and do provide others.

Aristotle would encourage the right kind of person to pursue political science, not so much for what it might do for others, but for its own intrinsic rewards, that is, as a mode of self-perfection. What kind of person should pursue political science? The study of political science will be a mode of self-perfection only for those who can truly enjoy the dark comedy of politics, where just causes are compromised by the quest for power and where noble intentions usually fail or lead to unintended and ignoble outcomes; and yet politics is also the arena where power at least

---

83. In the Politics Book II, Aristotle criticizes several (of what he takes to be) theoretical programs for political reform.

pretends to be justice, where what is merely *de facto* usually strives to be *de jure*. Politics is a twilight zone between right and might, between what is and what ought to be, between philosophical ideal and empirical reality. The study of politics is not for the squeamish: utopian idealism is usually a short road to self-destructive cynicism; but neither is the study of politics for the hard-nosed and value-free positivist, who cannot possibly grasp the moral irony of the human drama under investigation. Political science is likely to be fulfilling only for those with a high degree of tolerance for human foibles, for those who can accept the inevitable mixture of high aspirations and low interests, and for those who prefer justice incarnate to either abstract ideals or the play of brute forces.

The ultimate reward of the study of politics is the adventure of self-discovery. Aristotle says that practical science is a route to self-understanding in a way that the theoretical and technical sciences are not.[84] Why? Because in the encounter with other and very different modes of human self-realization, we discover ourselves in what we share and do not share with those others. The contemporary study of physics or engineering does not engage our deepest commitments and aspirations because we do not see ourselves in the object of inquiry; the investigation or manipulation of brute nature is not likely to cause us to discover or seek to change who we are because nature does not talk back and challenge our own self-conceptions. The study of political affairs, by contrast, is not or at least ought not to be merely the study of facts and theories that we learn and then forget; rather, political inquiry should lead to the kind of knowledge we gain from friendship, marriage, or parenting — knowledge that cannot be forgotten, knowledge that transforms us through new levels of self

---

84. Aristotle, Nicomachean Ethics 1141b 29ff.

awareness. As we imaginatively take sides in political controversies, as we wonder how human beings can come to think and act in such strange ways, as we ponder the strange admixture of good and ill, the risks and the rewards of political commitments and decisions, we can learn much about what we gain and lose through our own commitments and choices. Indeed, if we are open to the dynamics of self-understanding in the study of political affairs we might become quite different persons.

4. Bildungspolitik and the Claims of Sovereignty.

As we have seen, Aristotle understands politics and the state in terms of the full realization of the capacities of the citizens for intellectual and moral virtue. Liberty, equality, law, order, and wealth are all subordinated to this aspiration. The political community, on his account, is a community of communities, and includes families, villages, and other associations; every community exercises authority in proportion to its capacity to promote human development and happiness. But only the state is large and complex enough to afford a full-range of opportunities for a complete human life. It is this claim of the state to be a complete or perfect community that grounds and justifies the state's claim to plenary or sovereign authority.

Now it may very well be that the Athenian polis was never truly the self-sufficient or complete community of Aristotelian theory. The Athenian polis was always embedded in various religious, military, and commercial leagues with other Greek poleis as well as with its colonies. And Athenian intellectual life had always depended upon the stimulus of foreigners such as Aristotle himself. Aristotle says almost nothing about Athenian "international relations" but we know that they were extensive enough to sharply qualify any claims that Athens was self-sufficient. In some ways, the early modern nation-state might be said to have a better claim to self-sufficiency than the much smaller ancient polis – though nation-states have always been embedded in various international schemes for commercial, religious, cultural, and military cooperation. Today, scientific, scholarly, artistic, educational, commercial or military excellence is unthinkable apart from global cooperation. Even the nation-state must surrender its claim to be a perfect society: only the globe itself affords an arena large and complex enough for full human self-realization. If this is true, then Aristotle would expect that the nation-state would have to yield its claim to sovereign authority as well.

When nation-states transfer bits and pieces of their plenary authority to regional or global trade and financial organizations, military alliances, or legal institutions, we often describe this process in terms of a desire for greater prosperity, security, and lawfulness. Aristotle challenges us to consider all these complex new configurations of internationalized authority as so many facets of one underlying reality – that today, human flourishing requires a global arena. In the drama of the quest for human excellence, all the world must be a stage. More precisely, on Aristotle's account, human flourishing requires a range of arenas: while medical research requires global cooperation, political participation seems to flourish better on a much smaller scale. If human flourishing, then, requires a range of communities of varying scales, we should not be surprised to find the contemporary nation-state increasingly transferring its plenary powers both down to smaller communities and up to larger ones. Whether the drama of human self-realization takes a tragic or a comic turn will depend upon our success in distributing authority to various communities in proportion to their capacity to promote that self-realization.

Sovereignty and Rights in Medieval and Early Modern Jurisprudence: Law and Norms without a State

Kenneth Pennington

Beginning in the eleventh century, European legal systems made the slow transition from customary, largely unwritten, law to legal systems in which law was incorporated into the written word. During this period, laws and customs were not only written down, but jurists began to comment on them systematically. The result was that Europe experienced a remarkable rebirth of jurisprudence after 500 years of being a land without jurists. The main institutional basis of this revival was the teaching of ancient Roman law, and afterwards, canon law, in the schools of Italy.

The first center of legal studies was Bologna.[1] Pepo, Irnerius, and others begin to explicate the Emperor Justinian's (535-565 A.D.) sixth-century compilation of Roman law, the Cor-

---

1. The most recent and sophisticated history of the study of law in the twelfth century is Ennio Cortese, Il rinascimento giuridico medievale (Roma: Bulzoni Editore, 1992) with extensive bibliography to previous literature in English, German, and French. Some scholars have argued that Pavia preceded Bologna as a center for the study of law, but Cortese and most scholars do not find their arguments convincing. On the influence of the schools on general culture in the twelfth and thirteenth centuries see the superb chapter by Jürgen Miethke, De potestate papae: Die päpstliche Amtskompetenz im Widerstreit der politischen Theorie von Thomas von Aquin bis Wilhelm von Ockham (Spätmittelalter und Reformation, 16; Tübingen 2000) 1-24, on the influence of the new universities on European intellectual life.

pus iuris civilis, significant parts of which had lain dormant and unused during the intervening five centuries. Justinian's Corpus iuris civilis became the libri legales, the textbooks that new schools of law used during the twelfth century. These libri legales became the cornerstones of a new jurisprudence.

A shadowy figure named Gratian compiled a liber legalis for ecclesiastical law at the beginning of the twelfth century. Although the full story is not yet completely known, Gratian began to compile his book in the early twelfth century, perhaps as early as 1120, and by 1140-1160, his book was being used as the fundamental compilation of canon law all over Europe.[2] By the first decades of thirteenth century, Gratian's book was supplemented by a large number of books that collected papal case law, the decretals. Papal case law provided a rich and varied set of problems that the jurists explored in their commentaries and in the classroom.

As a consequence of the establishment of authoritative libri legales, law became an academic and intellectual discipline in a very short time. Student demand was great. Knowledge of law became economic coin. Law schools began to pullulate in Italy, Southern France, and Spain during the twelfth and thirteenth centuries. The curriculum was exactly the same everywhere: Justinian's Corpus iuris civilis and Gratian's Concordia discordantium canonum, or, as it was more commonly called, the Decretum, with papal decretals. As the study of law became entrenched in the schools of Europe, students began to study and to receive degrees in both laws: They became 'Doctores utriusque iuris.'

The jurists called the body of law that they studied, Roman

---

2. Anders Winroth, The Making of Gratian's Decretum (Cambridge-New York 2001).

and canon law, the Ius commune. It became the universal law of Europe from the early twelfth to the seventeenth century. During the reign of the Ius commune, teachers in the law schools throughout Europe not only used the same libri legales in their classrooms; they also used the same language of instruction: Latin. This lingua franca guaranteed that the focus of the law was universal and not particular. Liberated from the linguistic borders that limit intellectual horizons today, medieval students could attend any law school in Europe. One consequence of the schools' curriculum was that they did not teach local customary or statutory law. And although the schools were regulated by the Church in the early centuries, they were largely independent of the authority of the local prince.[3]

The institutional structure of the law schools had profound effects on law. Unlike today, the schools and the jurists who taught in them were not isolated geographically and jurisdictionally from each other. Although the law schools in Southern Europe were much more important and played a much larger role than the Northern schools during the twelfth and thirteenth centuries, the libri legales created a homogeneous curriculum that formed the foundation of every jurist's training. The jurists of the North read and taught the jurists of the South. The jurists of the South, especially those from the Iberian peninsula, Southern and Central France, and Italy produced an astounding amount of literature in several different genres. The result of this work was the development of a common European jurisprudence that emerged during the thirteenth century.

This jurisprudence transcended local law, the Ius proprium.

---

3. Manlio Bellomo, The Common Legal Past of Europe, 1000-1800 (Studies in Medieval and Early Modern Canon Law 4, Washington, D.C. 1995), discusses the history of the Ius commune and its significance for Western European jurisprudence.

From the late twelfth-century on, the jurists of the Ius commune developed a jurisprudence in which they attempted to isolate norms that had general application. Brian Tierney has recently demonstrated that these jurists explored rights of individuals systematically and developed a new language in which rights of human beings were discussed from many different perspectives.[4] In their commentaries and their teaching they created jurisprudential norms that protected those rights. As these jurisprudential norms were received in the classrooms, courts, and commentaries, they became more than legal maxims or legal rules: they became statements of equity and justice that ruled the world of thought and the world of the courts.

Today the sovereignty of the state protects the rights of citizens. In the era of the Ius commune, the rights of subjects were not, for the most part, protected by local customary law or statutory law.[5] Today individual rights are embedded in legislation, court decisions, and the constitutions of sovereign states. In the world of the Ius commune, the rights of subjects can be found in the writings of the jurists whose intricate arguments were conducted over centuries. In their thought they constructed these rights primarily by limiting the sovereignty of the prince. As

---

4. Brian Tierney, The Idea of Natural Rights: Studies on Natural Rights, Natural Law and Church Law 1150-1625 (Emory University Studies in Law and Religion; Atlanta, Georgia: 1997). For a discussion of how modern thinking about rights differs from medieval, see Richard H. Helmholz, "Natural Human Rights: The Perspective of the *Ius commune*", Catholic University Law Review 52 (2003) 301-325.

5. Richard Helmholz has argued that even Magna Carta borrowed many of its concepts from the Ius commune in "Magna Carta and the ius commune", The University of Chicago Law Review 66 (1999) 297-371. See also my "The Ius commune, Suretyship, and Magna carta," Rivista internazionale di diritto comune 11 (2000) 255-274

consensus evolved among the jurists, sometimes over centuries, about which rights were universal and which were not, the results became a part of the literature of the Ius commune. Consequently, during the Middle Ages and well into the early modern period, the jurisprudence of the Ius commune functioned as a constitution in which individual rights were detailed, explained, recognized, and asserted by generation after generation of jurists.

The "constitution" that the jurists fashioned was not limited by political and legal boundaries. Since the law schools in which the Ius commune was taught, studied, and interpreted were not a part of any territorial state and were not linked to any local legal system, it was a legal system without a state, an idea that is almost inconceivable in the world of the modern state system.

One of the main contributions of medieval and early modern Catholic jurisprudence (the Ius commune) was the establishment of individual rights as the foundation of its thinking about sovereignty. As Tierney's work has shown, a clear doctrine of individual and inalienable rights first surfaced in Western legal thought in the twelfth and thirteenth centuries. Political systems were not democratic, politics were not liberal, but jurists had a common set of norms to which they gave their consent. These norms were the building blocks upon which they constructed rights of property, obligations, marriage, defense, and due process. Today these rights are often protected against arbitrary magistrates of the sovereign state by constitutions. However, although constitutions may function as higher norms, their provisions can be changed, or, as we have seen in the late twentieth century, the political societies that had created them may disappear. In any case, the rights they protect cannot be considered eternal or inalienable.

In the bleak and sorry history of the twentieth century, individual rights and the sovereignty of the nation state have waged almost constant war against each other. Today they continue to do battle. Since the Convention for the Protection of Human Rights and Freedoms was adopted by sixteen European countries on November 4, 1950, human rights have been endorsed by heads of government, ratified by treaties, and violated by almost everyone. The culprit is the modern sovereign state, which recognizes the right of its citizens to act contrary to its will and its self-interest only with excruciating difficulty. The norms of the Ius commune created a much more stalwart defense of individual rights than we find in modern jurisprudence. The reason is that individual rights were embedded in a disinterested body of jurisprudence that was not susceptible to the argument that rights should be suspended because of "national interest or national self-preservation."

Unlike the rights granted by modern states to their citizens, the conceptions of sovereignty held by jurists of the Ius commune protected the rights of individuals — in many cases absolutely. The origins of the right to due process is a splendid example.[6] At the beginning of the thirteenth century, a defendant did not have the absolute right of due process. A judge or the prince could condemn a person without a trial. During the thirteenth century the jurists began to explore and debate the rights of defendants. By the end of the century they had reached a consensus that a defendant's right to a trial was grounded in natural law and, consequently, was inviolable. The most sophisticated and complete summing up of juristic thinking about the rights of defendants in the late thirteenth and early fourteenth centuries can be found in the work of a French

---

6. The following paragraphs are based on my The Prince and the Law: Sovereignty and Rights in the Western Legal Tradition (Berkeley-Los Angeles-London 1993) 119-164 and "Due Process, Community, and the Prince in the Evolution of the Ordo iudiciarius," Rivista internazionale di diritto comune 9 (1998) 9-47.

canonist, Johannes Monachus who died in 1313. While glossing a decretal of Pope Boniface VIII (Rem non novam) he commented extensively on defendants' rights. He began by asking the question: could the pope, on the basis of this decretal, proceed against a person if he had not cited him? Johannes concluded that the pope was only above positive law, not natural law. Since a summons had been established by natural law, the pope could not omit it. He argued that no judge, even the pope, could come to a just decision unless the defendant was present in court. When a crime is notorious, the judge may proceed in a summary fashion in some parts of the process, but the summons and judgment must be observed. He argued that a summons to court (citatio) and a judgment (sententia) were integral parts of the judicial process because Genesis 3.12 proved that both were necessary. God had been bound to summon Adam; human judges must do the same. Then he formulated an expression of a defendant's right to a trial and to due process with the following words: a person is presumed innocent until proven guilty (item quilbet presumitur innocens nisi probetur nocens).[7]

This sentence of Johannes Monachus has a delicious irony for anyone who has studied and read the literature on due process in English and American common law: rather than a sturdy, virtuous Anglo-Saxon, a cardinal of the Roman church, a Frenchman, a canonist, Johannes Monachus was the first European jurist to recognize the inexorable logic of God's judgment of Adam: God could not condemn Adam without a trial because even God must presume that Adam was innocent until proven guilty. The Old Testament provided yet another source from which jurists derived

---

7. See my "Innocent Until Proven Guilty: The Origins of a Legal Maxim," A Ennio Cortese (Roma: 2001) volume 3.

their norms.[8]

After Johannes, other canonists played with the idea of defendants' rights. They coined a proverb that God must even give the devil his day in court. Johannes' commentary on Rem non novam eventually became the Ordinary Gloss of a late medieval collection of canon law known as the Extravagantes communes. This collection and its gloss circulated in hundreds of manuscripts and scores of printed editions until the seventeenth century. Since his gloss was read by the jurists of the Ius commune until the eighteenth century, it was a primary vehicle for transmitting the principle of due process to later generations of jurists.

In the jurisprudence of the Ius commune, the maxim, "Innocent until proven guilty" summarized a bundle of rights that every human being should have, no matter what the person's status, religion, or citizenship. The maxim protected defendants from being coerced to give testimony and to incriminate themselves. It granted them the absolute right to be summoned, to have their case heard in an open court, to have legal counsel, to have their sentence pronounced publically, and to present evidence in their defense. A jurist of the Ius commune would be puzzled that today we can embrace the maxim "a person is innocent until proven guilty" and still deny human beings a judicial hearing under certain circumstances. For them the maxim meant "no one, absolutely no one, can be denied a trial under any circumstances." And that everyone, absolutely everyone, had the right to conduct a vigorous, thorough defense.

This tradition of thinking about rights survived into the early modern period. Since the recent work of Brian Tierney, we

---

8. See Richard Helmholz, The Spirit of Classical Canon Law (The Spirit of the Laws; Athens, Georgia-London: 1996) 41-42, 149-151, 164-165, 314-315, 344-347 et passim.

know that the sixteenth and seventeenth centuries were crucial for the development of a tradition of rights thinking in the European tradition. The most important event that challenged the jurists to continue thinking about individual rights was the discovery of the New World and new peoples in the sixteenth century. If a number of Spanish thinkers had not been confronted by this new set of problems, rights could have withered on the vine.[9]

    Certainly the sixteenth and seventeenth centuries were not great ages for human freedom in other areas. The doctrine of absolutism became acceptable coin of public political discourse, religious intolerance reached abysmal depths never before seen, censorship became a tool of European secular and religious regimes to control thought, witches were discovered in every crack and crevice, puritanism became the first and most important virtue that was added to the other seven: this list could be extended almost endlessly. Yet the discovery of lands populated with pagan peoples sparked a debate about their rights. Some of the best minds of the sixteenth century asked hard questions: Could native peoples have a just title to their lands? Could their lands be taken from them? Could they be enslaved? Francisco de Vitoria, Bartolomé de Las Casas, Francisco Suárez, and Hugo Grotius exploited the earlier traditions that they found in theology and in the Ius commune. They preserved the concept of rights in an age in which authoritarian power seems to have pride of place. Most readers know that these theologians and jurists defended the rights of indigenous peoples against the depredations of the sovereign state — their state. They used the norms of the Ius commune to argue for those rights. In the end the law failed indigenous native American peoples. Only recently have we begun to recognize, belatedly,

---

9. Tierney, Idea of Natural Rights 255-287.

the justice of these Spaniards' arguments.

The thought of a less well-known seventeenth-century Spanish jurist, Emanuel Gonzalez Tellez, demonstrates how deeply embedded "rights thinking" was in the minds of the jurists of the Ius commune. His work also illustrates how European juris-prudence still exercised power and authority over the minds of jurists in every corner of Europe at a time when the nation state had already sounded Ius commune's death knell.[10] Tellez is a splendid example of the continuity of the Catholic legal tradition and its defense of individual rights against the sovereign power of the state. Tellez' major work was a long, detailed commentary on the Decretals of Gregory IX, a great law book of the thirteenth century. As far as I can tell, Tellez' commentary on the Decretals was one of the last massive canonistic commentaries to enjoy European wide distribution. He taught at Salamanca and died in 1649.[11]

I would like to begin my discussion of Tellez at an unlikely spot to talk about natural rights: in the title devoted to the translation of bishops in book one of the Decretals of Gregory IX. This title contains four decretals of Pope Innocent III dating from 1198 to 1200 in which the pope suppressed forever the rights of local churches to translate bishops without papal approval. Inno-cent declared in Quanto personam, the most important decretal in this title, that he claimed this power and authority over bishops because "he does not exercise the office of man, but of the true God on

---

10. See Manlio Bellomo's recent reflections on the death of the Ius commune in "Condividendo, rispondendo, aggiungendo: Riflessioni intorno al 'ius commune'," Rivista internazionale di diritto comune 11 (2000) 287-296.

11. Virtually nothing has been written about Tellez; see B. Alonso's article in Diccionario de historia eclesiastica de España (Madrid 1972) 2.1038-1039 and Schulte, Die Geschichte der Quellen und Literatur des canonischen Rechts (Stuttgart 1875; reprint Graz 1956) 3.742.

earth."[12]

This is a strange cupboard for a canonist to look for rights. Tellez, however, began his commentary by asserting that Quanto personam led to the following conclusion: "A bishop who transfers himself on his own authority from one church to another loses both offices" and listed a long series of authorities who supported this statement.[13] Then he proposed the contrary:[14]

> Truly the present decision is contrary to ius and natural liberty and cannot be held. For a disposition of ius that infringes upon natural liberty cannot be admitted. The present disposition infringes upon natural liberty and cannot be sustained. First we may prove the minor thesis: a disposition that anyone may not leave a certain place or a certain city infringes upon natural liberty.

Tellez cited a passage from Justinian's Roman law Digest in which Tryphonius (Sabinus) argued that everyone had the right (libera facultas) to choose his own city and Cicero that it is a foundation of liberty that no one may be forced to stay in a city unwillingly.[15]

---

12. On the importance of this decretal for Innocent's ecclesiology and for later political thought, see chapter 2 in my Pope and Bishops: The Papal Monarchy in the Twelfth and Thirteenth Centuries (Philadelphia 1984) 13-42, which is revised, augmented, and printed again in Popes, Canonists and Texts, 1150-1550 (Aldershot 1993).

13. Emanuelis Gonzalez Tellez, Commentaria perpetua (Venice: 1766) 1.240 to X 1.7.3.

14. Ibid.: "Verum praesens decisio ut juri et naturali libertati contraria, sustineri nequit; nam juris dispositio, per quam infringitur naturalis libertas, admitti non debet, sed praesens dispositio infringit naturalem libertatem, igitur sustineri non debet. Probatur minor, nam dispositio ut quis a tali loco vel civitate non recedat, infringit naturalem libertatem."

15. Ibid.: "De sua civitate statuendi facultas libera esse debet (ajebat Triphonius) in l. In bello 12. ff. de captivis (Dig. 49.15.12.9) et Cicero in Oratione pro

His last citation was to Hugo Grotius' De iure belli ac pacis libri tres.[16] Grotius had argued that although there were exceptions to the general rule, a person might leave his state. Although he cited the same passages from the Digest and Cicero, Grotius did not base his argument on a natural right to immigrate but on a concept of the common good. Tellez probably borrowed the citations from Grotius, but the Spaniard emphasized the absolute right of a person to move freely. Where Grotius saw a right circumscribed by the duties of persons to support the existence and well-being of the state, Tellez saw individual rights based on natural law.

Even more importantly for the argument of this paper is the fact that Tellez knew and had read Grotius' great treatise De iure belli. Grotius published his essay in 1625. We have known for a long time that the Dutch jurist read and cited contemporary Spanish, Italian, French, English, German and Dutch jurists and had also cited a remarkable number of jurists who had written their works from the twelfth to the sixteenth century. Even a casual reading of De iure belli will convince any reader that Grotius was influenced by, borrowed from, and contributed to the jurisprudence of the Ius commune. His Protestant religious convictions did not exclude the ideas of Catholic jurists. Renowned Spanish jurists and theologians like Francisco de Vitoria and Francisco Suarez, to-gether with much more obscure figures like Rodericus Suarez and Balthazar de

---

Balbo, laudat ius illud ne quis in civitate maneat invitus et vocat fundamentum libertatis." Cicero had written, Oratio pro Balbo § 31: "O iura praeclara atque divinitus iam inde a principio Romani nominis a maioribus nostris comparata, ne quis nostrum plus quam unius civitatis esse possit, — dissimilitudo enim civitatum varietatem iuris habeat necesse est, — ne quis invitus civitate mutetur neve in civitate maneat invitus! Haec sunt enim fundamenta firmissima nostrae libertatis, sui quemque iuris et retinendi et dimittendi esse dominum."

16. Ibid.: "Grotius, de iure belli, l.2, c.25 [recte 5], num. 24."

Ayala, dot the margins and inhabit the footnotes of his texts. These men inspired his thought and justified his convictions. Grotius may have been Protestant but in law he was catholic. In this respect, however, Grotius was not unusual. All the jurists of the Ius commune participated in a legal system without borders.

Conversely Tellez must have read Grotius within a decade or two after the publication of De iure belli. The Ius commune was a pan-European legal system, and its literature was universal. There were three reasons why. The first is language. From the twelfth to the seventeenth century, the language of the classrooms, the language of the standard texts, and the language of the literature that explicated the texts was Latin. The linguistic barriers between jurists that isolate them from one another today did not exist then. The second is the curriculum of the schools. Since the end of the twelfth century, the libri legales used in the law schools were the same all over Europe. Every student, whether in Oxford or Bologna, Salamanca or Prague, read the same texts. Professors taught those texts and read the same specialized literature. A Grotius was not separated from a Tellez by language, terminology, and intellectual background — or by religious belief. The result was a common set of presuppositions and an intellectual tradition that was not tainted by the parochial idiosyncrasies of local customs. The third reason is the invention of printing that allowed the works of these jurists to reach the far corners of Europe. The result was a common set of presuppositions and an intellectual tradition that was not tainted by the parochial idiosyncrasies of local customs. In particular their thinking was not limited by the norms of local custom.

Let us return, however, to Tellez and his argument that people had the natural right to move from place to place. In the end, he did not uphold the position that the bishop could move without papal authority. His ultimate conclusion conceded that since a bishop was married to his church this marriage bond took precedence over his natural liberty to move.[17] He noted that even though Robert Bellarmine and others had criticized translations in the modern church, they were still lawful.[18] Even though Tellez' argumentation was a part of a dialectic that did not carry the day, the point remains that by the seventeenth century jurists had been sensitized to the issues of the natural rights of human beings. Tellez conceded that bishops could not move without papal permission, but it is clear from his argument that he assumed that every other human being could move from place to place. Freedom to travel without interference was a basic human right, and the state could not violate those rights. It is not by chance that it was Tellez in the sixteenth century and not another earlier canonist who raised the problem of rights while commenting on Quanto personam. Jurists saw issues of rights in the seventeenth century in places where they had never noticed them before. Even Grotius, who was as attuned to the rights of individuals as any jurist of the Ius commune, did not grant persons the natural right and liberty of immigration.

---

17. On episcopal translations and earlier attitudes, see my Pope and Bishops: The Papal Monarchy in the Twelfth and Thirteenth Centuries (The Middle Ages; Philadelphia: University of Pennsylvania Press, 1984). Also Sebastian Scholz, Transmigration und Translation: Studien zum Bistumwechsel der Bischöfe von der Spätantike bis zum Hohen Mittelalter (Kölner Historische Abhandlungen, 37; Köln-Weimar-Wien: Böhlau Verlag, 1992) and Mary Sommar, The Changing Role of the Bishop in Society: Episcopal Translation in the Middle Ages (Ph.D. Syracuse University 1998).

18. Tellez, Commentaria, 1.240 to X 1.7.3: "Translationes etiam cum superioris auctoritate factas impugnaret Robertus Bellarminus, virtute et sapientia praeclarus, proposuit Clementi VIII. cuius verba refert Diana . . . et nostris temporibus non minus graviter et eleganter illustrissimus Fr. Joannes Martinez."

The modern state has restricted the rights of its subjects and others to move from place to place for the common good. Since the middle of the nineteenth century it has decided that its borders were sacrosanct and that it had the authority to infringe upon the natural liberty of people to move from one state to another. Tellez would have been puzzled. He thought that the right to immigrate was a natural right that had been recognized since Roman times. It was a norm of the Ius commune.

Another area of rights illustrates Tellez' attitudes: the right to bear arms. At the end of the eleventh century the church had moved broadly to forbid clerics from carrying arms. A canon from the Council of Poitiers in 1079 banning clergy from bearing arms became part of the normative law of the church by the late twelfth century.[19] But, from the beginning, the absolute interdiction of clerical arms was tempered by the canonists' notions of rights. They immediately interpreted the canon as excepting a cleric's right to self-defense. Between the thirteenth and the seventeenth centuries, the jurists distinguished between offensive and defensive weapons, dangerous and safe places, and a cleric's and a layman's right to defend himself. Tellez makes the old points. "Natural reason permits us to defend ourselves from danger . . . whence this ius, that one may repel arms with arms, is said to have been established from nature.[20] However, Tellez expands the scope of a cleric's rights to bear arms considerably. "No one should doubt," he wrote, "that in case of necessity clerics can defend themselves

---

19. X 3.1.2.

20. Tellez, Commentaria to X 3.1.2, vol. 3, p.6: "et ipsa naturalis ratio permittat ut a periculis nos defendamus, l. Itaque 4. ff. de iustitia et iure (Dig. 1.1.3), unde ius hoc, ut arma armis repellere liceat, a natura comparatum dicitur, l.1 § Vim vi 27 ff. de vi et vi armat (Dig. 43.16[15]).

from force and also defend their homeland."[21] "If a city is attacked by enemies, a cleric may take up arms for reasons of defense."[22] To this point Tellez endorses a cleric's right to bear arms that is congruent with the thought of other jurists during the sixteenth and seventeenth centuries.

What sets Tellez apart from his predecessors is the last part of his commentary. Here he turned, naturally, it seems, to the rights of laymen to bear arms. His point of departure is a statute in Justinian's Code of Roman statutes that forbade any Roman from bearing arms without the permission of the emperor.[23] Tellez observes that a large number of jurists from Bartolus to Socinus understood this text as banning citizens from bearing arms.[24] The great proceduralist of the late sixteenth and early seventeenth century, Prospero Farinacci, concluded that those who bore arms in public became liable to a "mala praesumptio."[25] Tellez wrote a long essay on the historical origins of the Roman statute and concluded that it was not a general prohibition from bearing arms. Consequently, Bartolus and others did not understand the text

---

21. Ibid. p. 7: "Nec obstat dubitandi ratio supra expensa nam a praesenti generali prohibitione necessitatis casus excipiendi sunt ut contra vim tum sibi tum patriae illatuam armis sese clerici defendere possint."

22. Ibid.: "Eadem ratione si civitas ab hostibus oppugnatur, clerici arma defensionis causa sumere possunt."

23. Cod. 11.47 (46)1: "Nulli prorsus nobis insciis atque inconsultis quorumlibet armorum movendorum copia tribuatur."

24. Bartolus, Commentaria to Dig. 48.6.1 (Venice 1526), fol. 188v.

25. Prospero Farinacci, (Prosperus Farinacius), Praxis et theoricae criminalis libri duo in quinque titulos distributi (Frankfurt 1606) Liber 1, tit. 5, quaestio 52, p. 796, num 70: "Regula itaque ex praemissis firma remanet quod ex delatione armorum oritur contra deferentem indicium et mala praesumptio. Et hoc, quia armorum usus regulariter a iure prohibitus est."

correctly. For just and honest reasons, private citizens may bear arms.[26] I would like to think that Tellez might have changed his mind if faced with 250 million handguns in the US, but I also think that this discussion illustrates how he saw issues of rights to which earlier generations of jurists were oblivious. Most importantly he firmly believed, as all of his predecessors had believed, that the sovereign state could not abrogate or derogate rights that were protected by higher norms. These norms transcended the positive law of the state.

The language of rights, based on the jurisprudential norms of the Ius commune, permeates Tellez' commentary. In his commentary on the Fourth Lateran canon prohibiting Christians from selling arms to Moslems, Tellez again raises the issue of rights.[27] How could the Church, he asked, forbid Christians to buy or sell goods when contracts of sale and purchase are part of the natural law?[28] Furthermore, since the Fourth Lateran canon decreed those Christians who commanded ships in the Moslem fleets could be enslaved if they were captured by Christians, Tellez pointed out that since liberty is a natural ius, positive law could not derogate natural law.[29] As in his discussion of episcopal translations, Tellez

---

26. Tellez, loc. cit. p.8: "ex justa et honest causa liceat privatis arma deferre."

27. Tellez to X 5.6.6, vol. 5, p. 91.

28. Ibid. p. 92: "Sed pro dubitandi ratione ita in praesentem assertionem insurgo! Contractus praecipue emptionis et venditionis juris naturalis secundarii, quod alii jus gentium appellant, sunt . . .Igitur Ecclesia non potuit prohibere venditionem armorum et caeterarum mercium, de quibus in praesenti, Saracenis seu Infidelibus, neque transitus aut navigatio contra societatis humanae et Christianae charitatis regulas prohiberi debet."

29. Ibid.: "Etiam difficilis est praesens constitutio in poena quam imponit Christianis suscipientibus regimen navium, videlicet ut capientium servi fiant,

raises objections to the Lateran decree based on natural law and natural rights but in the end concedes that the church or the secular prince can restrict these rights. The selling of arms to enemies and the enslavement of freemen can, under certain circumstances, be tolerated. What is important for our purposes is the language of rights with which he framed his contrarietates. But as in his commentary on the right of clerics to bear arms, here too he steps beyond his text to discuss the right of the prince to ban commerce. Princes may forbid their subjects to engage in commerce under certain conditions, but they may not ban commerce absolutely. The language of his conclusions is worth quoting:[30]

> For although contracts of sale and purchase are part of the ius gentium, and although princes may not prohibit their subjects absolutely, they can prohibit similar commerce with just cause for some people or of some things, because such a prohibition is supported by a more powerful natural reason, as Albericus Gentilis has noted. The ius of commerce is a ius founded on equity (ius aequum is untranslatable but has a rich resonance in the jurisprudence of the Ius commune) and defending safety is accomplished more justly with equity. The law of commerce is just but (the law) of preserving safety is more just. The former is based

---

nam libertas juris naturalis est . . . ergo lege positiva contra jus naturale servitus constitui non potest."

30. Ibid: "nam licet contractus emptionis et venditionis jus gentium sit, et ideo principes absolute subditis illum prohibere non possint, tamen respectu aliquarum personarum seu rerum ex justis causis simile commercium interdicere valent, quia talis prohibitio nititur potentiori naturalique ratione, nam ut inquit Alb. Gentil. l.1 de jure belli, c.21, jus commerciorum aequum est; at aequius tuendae salutis est. Illud gentium jus, hoc naturae est. Illud privatorum est, hoc regnorum. Cedat igitur regno mercatura, homo naturae, pecunia vitae, ut prosequitur Arniseus, l.1 de repub. cap. 3., sect. 3."

on the law of nations, the latter on that of nature. The former is the concern of private persons, the latter of kingdoms. So commerce yields to the kingdom, man to nature, money to life.

I cannot leave Tellez without looking at a place where one would expect to find the language of rights in full regalia: the chapter on theft in the Decretals of Gregory IX upon which the canonists, beginning in the twelfth century, had built a fortress defending the rights of the poor.[31] Tierney first wrote about this chapter in *Medieval Poor Law*.[32] He returned to it again in *The Idea of Natural Rights*.[33] This text and others in the Decretum spawned what Tierney describes as a "rightful power" or a "rightful claim" of the poor to the goods of society and is a prickly piece of evidence that even the most skeptical critics must choke on if they wish to deny that the medieval jurists did not have any conception of a natural right. What did Tellez add to five centuries of commentary on this text? For the most part, he repeated the standard interpretations: Theft of food or clothing when driven by the necessity of hunger or nudity was not a crime or a sin. Not even a penance could be imposed on a person. The common principle was, Necessity made licit what otherwise was illicit. Necessity makes all property common. According to natural law, all property is held in common; natural law cannot be derogated in times of necessity under any circumstances.[34] Tellez could have written the same words if he had lived in the thirteenth century. Only at the end of his commentary did he depart from the standard

---

31. X 5.18.3.

32. Medieval Poor Law: 37-38.

33. Natural Rights 73.

34. Tellez, Commentaria to X 5.18.3, vol. 5, p. 212.

commentary. Could a starving person eat food that had been sacrificed to idols? A text in Gratian's Decretum seems to forbid it. Tellez concludes:[35]

> Nevertheless the urgent necessity of hunger permits them to eat it. The command to preserve life is a part of natural law (here one may argue whether we should translate this passage as "natural law" or "natural right") and the prohibition is only a part of positive law. When two precepts conflict, one of natural law and one of positive law, natural law always prevails.

However, if a Christian were forced to eat as a part of the cult's liturgy, then Tellez agreed with Vitoria: the person should rather die than eat.[36] The natural rights of human beings do have their limits.

The Ius commune of the sixteenth and seventeenth centuries is important for our world because it directly links our ideas and thinking about rights to the ideas of medieval and early modern jurists and theologians. The main conduit though which the concept of natural rights flowed was not another theologian, but the Dutch Protestant jurist, Hugo Grotius (1583-1645). In De jure belli, Grotius grappled with the meanings of right (ius) in all of its multifarious meanings. I was surprised that Grotius, who died four years before him, influenced Tellez. I should not have been. It

---

35. Ibid: "tamen urgente famis necessitate licet illis vesci, quia cum praeceptum vitae conservandae sit juris naturalis, prohibitio autem illa tantum sit juris positivi, ideo quando duo praecepta simul concurrunt, quorum unum est juris naturalis, aliud vero juris positivi, juri naturali quod praevalet."

36. Ibid.: "Si autem cogatur quis idolothytis vesci in idolorum cultum, tunc procedit textus in Decreto, c. Sicut satis (C.32. q.4 c.8), quia potius debet pati mortem quam idolatriae consentire, ut docuerunt Victoria in relect. de usu cibor. n.3 Acunna in cap. Presbiter, num. fin. 50 dist.."

demonstrates, once again, two of the central points in this paper: how open the intellectual world of jurisprudence still was in the seventeenth century and how pervasive the language of rights was in that world.

The three elements that were central to the jurisprudence of the Ius commune in its waning years were its norms, its concept of natural law and of natural rights. Tellez, Grotius, and the other jurists thought these norms often trumped the sovereignty of the state, except under certain circumstances when other, usually collective, rights trumped individual rights. The jurisprudence of the Ius commune was the Träger of individual rights. It protected the rights of individual across territorial and jurisdictional borders. It protected rights without the state.

Of equal importance, however, was the vehicle through which the Ius commune was created. From the twelfth century the law schools provided the crucial institutional context that nurtured the evolution of a humane jurisprudence. It is impossible to imagine that the Ius commune would have evolved if the schools had been linked to the law of a certain territory. Jurists were not isolated from one another. They conducted long, sophisticated discussions with their contemporaries and their predecessors in their teaching and their works. The result was a jurisprudence that protected the rights of persons as well as any legal system in the modern world and better than most.

A legal and an educational system that is independent of national, religious, and ethnic blinders would be difficult, perhaps impossible, to establish in our fragmented world. The model of the Ius commune, nonetheless, provides us with a rich realm of ideas and possibilities. It created a jurisprudence and a set of norms that was the product of centuries of debate in the classroom, in the pages of books, in the courtroom, and in the chambers of legislative authority. Recently I discovered that a famous voice from the past, Alessandro Manzoni, had partially made my main point several centuries ago. In the debate over the use of torture in criminal proceedings Manzoni had pointed out that Pietro Verri had overemphasized his contribution to the intellectual arguments that underpinned his condemnation of torture and de-emphasized the contribution of earlier jurists. As part of Manzoni's account of a Milanese cause célèbre in which the judges sent several innocent men to the rack with almost no evidence of their guilt, he demonstrated that Verri had seriously distorted the legal tradition when he emphasized the novelty and orginality of his own thought:[37]

> From this evidence and from all we know of the practice of torture in their own time, one can undoubtedly conclude that the interpreters of criminal procedure left the theory and practice of torture much, but much, less barbarous than they found it. Of course it would be absurd to attribute this diminution of evil to one cause alone, but I think that among the many causes that it would be reasonable to count the repeated reproofs and warnings, renewed publicly, century after century, by jurists to whom it certainly

---

37. Alessandro Manzoni, Storia della colonna infame: Testo del 1840, ed. Alberto Chiari and Fausto Ghisalberti (Verona 1963) 702: "Da queste testimonianze, e da quello che sappiamo essere stata la tortura negli ultimi suoi tempi, si può francamente dedurre che i criminalisti interpreti la lasciarono molto, ma molto, men barbara di quello che l'avevan trovata. E certo sarebbe assurdo l'attribuire a una sola causa una tal diminuzione di male; ma, tra le molte, me par che sarebbe anche cosa poco ragionevole il non contare il biasimo e le ammonizioni ripetute e rinnovare pubblicamente, di secolo in secolo, da quelli ai quali pure s'attribuisce un'autorità di fatto sulla practica de' tribunali." Manzoni's father was probably Giovanni Verri, the brother of Pietro, and his mother was Giulia Beccaria, the daughter of Cesare, see Alessandro Manzoni, Storia della colonna infame: Testo definitivo e prima redazione, ed. Renzo Negri (Milano 1974) 5.

can be granted a definite authority over the practice of the courts.

Manzoni had extraordinary insight into how the norms governing torture evolved in European jurisprudence. He understood the complicated dialectic through which jurists argued with, borrowed from, and added to the thought of their predecessors and, in their works, spoke across the centuries to their successors. He also understood that the thought of the jurists eventually penetrated into the rough and tumble of the courtroom.

Today Europe seeks a new Ius commune and a new constitution. The world seeks a jurisprudence that will protect the rights of all human beings much more effectively than the nation state has done over the past two centuries. Although the liberal, democratic state has made great progress since the eighteenth century there is not a single one that has not seriously and shamefully violated the rights of its citizens and its non-citizens in the name of self-preservation during the past fifty years. The necessities and dangers of the moment have almost always provided governments with an excuse to infringe upon individual rights. If we take the Ius commune as a model for the modern world in which legal systems and human beings are held hostage to the needs of states, we might conclude that law is too precious a commodity to be left in the hands of bureaucrats, politicians, legislators, and, most importantly, those leaders who privilege the existence and prerogatives of their territorial states at the expense of their citizens.

In a recent column George F. Will, an American conservative political commentator, assured his readers that:

> A proper constitution distributes power among legislative, executive and judicial institutions so that the will of the majority can be measured, expressed in policy and, for the protection of minorities, somewhat limited. A proper con-

stitution does not give canonical status, as rights elevated beyond debate, to policy preferences of the moment.[38] Will's certainty is wrapped in historical ignorance. The Framers of the American Constitution quickly realized that when they had "distributed power among legislative, executive and judicial" branches of government, they had omitted to limit the power of the government to oppress the American people. They tried to remedy their omission with the Bill of Rights. The list of rights that they included is a potpourri. Some spoke to the "policy preferences of the moment"[39] and others expressed norms that had been entrenched in the law for centuries. As I demonstrated earlier the right of due process that was incorporated into the Fifth Amendment had a long history in the jurisprudence of the Ius commune. It is worth pondering that the right of due process has been systematically weakened rather than strengthened since its inclusion into the American Constitution. And at this moment (2003) it is under a sustained siege in the United States. The American war on terrorism has clearly demonstrated that political leaders, judges, jurists, and political commentators like Will feel free to strip defendants of their rights even if these rights are embedded in a Constitution. The Fifth Amendment states that "no person can be deprived of life, liberty, or property without due process of law". The American Supreme Court has flouted the clear intent and language of the amendment by limiting the right of due process to American citizens. In its present war on terrorism the government has even stripped its citizens of that fundamental right.[40]

---

38. Washington Post (July 27, 2003).

39. E.g. Sections of Amendments 1, 2, 3.

40. The United States Supreme Court recognized the rights of non-citizend to due process in the courts and for the first time in 2001 and seemed to

George F. Will's view on what is a "proper constitution" are not limited to his end of the political spectrum. Constitutional lawyers concentrate on "preferences of the moment" that the Framers of the American Constitution had chosen and ignore the rich jurisprudence that shaped those preferences. States have always and will always attempt to take away the rights of persons living within their boundaries. I would argue that a jurisprudence with roots sunk deeply in the long tradition of human experience and not limited by linguistic, political, cultural, and legal boundaries provides the best hope for a "proper constitution" that will respect the rights of all human beings.

---

acknowledge that non-citizens have the same constitutional rights as citizens. In two decisions, *Immigration and Naturalization Service v. St. Cyr* and *Zadvydas v. Davis*, the court held that non-citizens should be extended rights of due process. Johannes Monachus would have been shocked that this would even be an issue 700 years after he wrote. As David Cole wrote in *The New York Times* (July 1, 2001): "Yet in two surprising decisions handed down last week, the Supreme Court has come close to recognizing that immigrants are persons entitled to the same basic constitutional protections that apply to citizens. In doing so, the court broke from its own ignoble history of slighting immigrant's interests and may well have embarked on a new era in immigrants' rights."

Unfortunately the Supreme Court of the United States took a major step backwards in their decision of *DeMore v. Kim* (April 2003). As Davis Cole wrote in *The Washington Post* (May 7, 2003) the decision held that "the constitutional guarantee of due process means something different for a non-citizen than for a citizen, thus reneging on its own statement to years earlier that the due process clause does not 'acknowledge any distinction between citizens and resident aliens'."

Universalism and Particularism according to Francisco Suárez

Norbert Brieskorn SJ

"Rethinking the State" is our topic here. For this purpose we assume that the conception of the nation state has changed radically, and equally its functions and its potentials. These changes have received widespread public attention in recent years. With a view to decreasing the obligations of governments, privatisation of state functions has been undertaken (as in the case of the German post office and railways), legitimized by the tradition of free-market liberalism and the idea of human rights. Given the increasing interrelation of states and the ever greater permeability of their borders, nowadays hardly any state can secure its territory solely by itself. Nor can a state today remain independent of international financial markets or avoid foreign cultural influences that more and more often lead to conflicts with domestic culture.

There is thus an ironic aptness in introducing Francisco Suárez'(1548-1617) thinking on the state, for the state sketched by Suárez was not unlike today's states. First of all, Suárez' state was at a stage of development that contemporary liberal states want to reach again: a point where the state confines itself to only a few functions. In this respect, Suárez' state is a long way from a welfare state. We also find in Suárez' theory of the state parallels to international developments affecting states today. Suárez' state finds itself under the spiritual influence of the supranational Church, an influence whose positive dynamics as well as limitations could only partly be counteracted by the state. Thus in the sixteenth and seventeenth centuries we can observe the kind of international influence that has always created intra-state and intra-cultural problems. Nor could one at that time clearly specify, as it is important in political theory to do, whether an institution was subordinate to a superior power of the same order. Because Suárez does not yet know a sovereign power superior to the state, he thinks of the state as sovereign. At the same time, he concedes an indirect power to the Pope, which then belongs to a different, non-state, spiritual order. (Defensio fidei. III. 3. and 23).[1] Although spiritual power cannot be equated with secular power, it intrudes into secular power when it asserts its right to remove the sovereign.[2]

In "De legibus" Suárez draws our attention to three insights, which I will try to sketch in this chapter. It is indispensable that there exist some kind of social institution wherever (a) a good number of individuals and families come together, (b) with their culturally influenced needs, (c) relying on the ability of this institution to answer those needs.

Although on one end of the organizational spectrum the family is insufficient as a social organization, yet on the other end there is in Suárez' thinking no need for strong, supra-national institutions. (To be sure, he does not exclude every single one of them.)[3] A suprafamilial entity of some kind is derived from the

---

Thanks are due to all participants in the Berlin conference (21-23 September 2000) for their questions and comments on this paper.

1. In his teaching about potestas indirecta Suárez acknowledges the spiritual power of the Pope over the Christian and the heretic sovereigns (e.g., over the King of England).
2. Soder 1973, 335f.; Scott, 267-270.
3. I agree on this point with Soder 1973, 231f.; cf. note 28 and 29.

nature of the union of men, not from the nature of man, though it always relies on man's activity as a founder and preserver. There will invariably be three functions for such an institution to fulfill: legislation, application of laws, and jurisprudence.

For Suárez the state always has the right to attack another state and to intervene in it, though this right applies under very strict conditions. Massive injustice has to be experienced, or intervention must be the only way to protect the lives of innocent people (De bello. V. 6; De fide. XVIII. 4. 4). Even the right to religious freedom justifies an intervention, though the right belongs only to believers in monotheistic religions (De bello. V. 3). Military means can also justly be invoked to guarantee the right to proclaim a faith and the general right of free access to information (De bello. V. 7 and 8; De fide. XVIII. 1. 4 and 2. 8). This does not include the obligation to accept a faith!

Suarez' thinking was also shaped by a special case, urgent in his own time, of the problem of "universalism and parti-cularism"; and some knowledge of this background will help us to understand his theory of the state. "Universalism and particularism" was a duality confronting the early Christian communities, living among the pagans and having a mission to all people. In this situation, a universal mission to mankind had to be undertaken by a minority dwelling among a non-Christian majority. Augustine took up this problem as a theologian of history when he sketched the "civitas dei" in the midst of the all encompassing "civitas terrena." So did Thomas Aquinas later on in his "Summa contra gentiles" – but not only there. Aquinas also reflected upon the individual in the light of the universal in such writings as his Summa Theologiae I-II. Quaest. 94. Art. 4 and II-II 57ff., together with "De regimine principum" etc.

The friars' reflections, shortly after the beginning of the sixteenth century, on colonisation, on titles of conquest and settlement, and on the treatment of the indigenous population lead us closer to our political topic (Antonio de Montesino, ca.1485-1540, Pedro de Córdoba 1482-1521, Pedro de Gante 1486-1572, Bartolomé de las Casas 1474-1566). John Maior, or Mair (1467-1550), opened the line of teachers reflecting on the variety of problems that arose as a result of the "discovery" of Christopher Columbus. Should Castilian law now apply world-wide, or was there a need to develop a new, supra-national law? Or – a third alternative – should the various local bodies of law be further developed? Was it not necessary to have standards that applied everywhere, that were thus universal, and that no one could evade? For example, on the one hand rights for all individuals, on the other hand protection of the Christian religion that had to be respected by everyone? Francisco de Vitoria (1480-1546) conducted these reflections on the high level for which he is well known as both a jurist and a theologian, beginning with "De potestate civili," dated Christmas 1528, to "De indis prior" and "De indis posterior seu de iure belli" in 1539.

Francisco Suárez (1548 - 1617), jurist, philosopher and theologian, followed in Vitoria's footsteps. "Although he never stood in the presence of the maestro Vitoria, he studied at Salamanca, and grew up in the famous Victorian tradition."[4] Suárez first voiced his own opinions in Rome in 1585, in the course of lecturing about "De iustitia et iure." Later on, he deepened his knowledge and increased the subtlety of his distinctions; the results were "De baptismo" in 1587, "De homicidio" and "De censuris" in 1592, and (at the University of Coimbra from 1600 onwards) "De opere sex dierum" (Book V). Finally he published "De legibus ac Deo legislatore" (DL) in 1612. Chapters 17 to 20 of the second

---

4. Scott, 129 (the text is adapted).

book of DL, concerning the ius gentium, and chapters 1 to 4 of the third book, discussing the ius civile, merit special interest. We have yet to mention the works "Defensio fidei," written in 1613, and "De triplici virtute theologica," published four years after Suárez' death in 1621.[5]

Two considerations should help us to understand better the Suárezian approach. First, in 1580 Portugal was unified with Spain, not to the great pleasure of the Portuguese. King Philip II asked Suárez to take over the chair of theology in the Portuguese University of Coimbra. The Society of Jesus accepted this appointment and sent him there. Suárez arrived in 1598 in an occupied country, very aware of the delicate situation and of the sensibilities of the Portuguese. Twice in the first two books of DL he warned of the danger of simply transferring Spanish legislation to Portugal without first discerning whether the law in question would fit into Portuguese legal culture.[6] Each part of the Iberian peninsula had its own law and a right to follow it.

The second remark concerns the difference between Vitoria and Suárez: "The philosophy of Victoria was [...] for an occasion, or rather to bring a concrete situation - arising from the discovery of the New World - within the law of Christendom, thus universalizing it. Whereas the purpose of Suárez was to state the universal law and its elements in the abstract, with sufficient reference to concrete instances to give it a substance and a body." And Suárez reached the goal: "the establishment of a single and universal standard of right and wrong in the relations of individuals within the state, in the relations of states with one another, and in the

---

5. Several theses concerning the position of Suárez can be found in the following works of Brouillard, Mesnard, Rommen and Scott.

6. DL. I. 7. No. 6 and No. 14.

international community composed of these individuals and of these states."[7]

With this background, let us now proceed to explore more specifically what Suárez had to say that might help us today to "rethink the state."

1. The Main Notions of *De Legibus ac Deo Legislatore*

Suárez' main concern is not the amelioration of world politics as it existed in the "world" of the sixteenth century; nor is he preoccupied with questions of values, structures, political bodies, groups, and institutions. His two questions are very clear: What exactly is the law, the ius, the law of nations, etc.? And how does it work?

He always starts with the question of existence: Is there really a law and a right (ius), etc.? In his reflections Suárez in the first place wants to reassure himself that the object of his reflections really exists (DL. II. 17. No. 1). And only because he was able to confirm that something like a ius gentium, a law of nations, already existed did he begin to reflect on it.

1.1 What is law? "Law is a measure of moral acts" or "a rule of action" (Prologue of DL; DL. I. 1 a. o.), "strictly and absolutely speaking, only that which is a measure of rectitude, viewed absolutely and consequently, is a right and virtuous rule."[8] Aquinas' definition of law is for Suárez "too broad and too gen-

---

7. Scott, 130.
8. For the following: Scott, 134 - 137.

eral"[9] because it includes rules for craftsmen and technical instructions as well as natural laws in the sense understood in political science today, and also what might be called pure advice [consilium]. For Suárez on the other hand "law" is a universal rule, relating to all persons, or to the majority, in due proportion; law is a common, just, and stable precept. "Common" in that it applies to all; "just" in that it is equitable and moral; "stable" in that it is permanent. And last, he stresses that it has to be promulgated (for the definition of law cf. DL. I. 12). The law (or the precept) contains inherently a cause to carry it into effect. The one without the other is incomplete, the law without the sanction. It is therefore the duty of every community to provide the sanction (DL. I. 3. No. 14 and III. 3 No. 1 and 5).[10]

We can see that in the law itself we meet the tension between universality and particularity. The mediation between these two is the task of the entire law, the aim of which is precisely to regulate a special case yet to put it under a rule and a general measure. And vice-versa, the law applies the universal rule to the concrete case.

1.2 And what is "ius"? In DL I. 2 we find many questions, comparisons and definitions to clarify the relation between "lex" and "ius." There are three main answers to the problem of this relationship, each depending on the content of the concepts "lex" and "ius." The first answer is that there is no difference at all. "Ius"

---

9. Aquinas: "Law is a species of rule and measure in accordance with which one is induced to act or is restrained from acting" (Sth. I - II. 90. Art. 1: Lex regula est quaedam et mensura actuum secundum quam inducitur aliquis ad agendum vel ab agendo retrahitur"); Suárez omits "actuum", which Aquinas has connected with "regula"; Scott 134.

10. DL. I. 9, III. 1. No. 10, III. 3. No.3 and III. 4. No. 4; Scott, 239.

means "law," and "ius" as the rule of righteous conduct that establishes a certain equity in things is exactly the "law" (DL. II. 17. No. 2). A second answer is that "ius" is broader than "lex." Suárez cites the example of "in ius vocari," "to be summoned before the [law-]court." "Ius" has a wider variety of meanings than simply "law" (DL. II. 14. No. 16 and II. 18. No. 2).

But Suárez follows the line of a third answer, that "ius" is "a moral faculty over or relating to something"; faculty "is a right in the sense that it involves the true dominion or merely a partial dominion, which faculty is, according to Aquinas, the true object of justice" (DL. I. 2, II. 14 No. 16 and II. 17. No. 2; DL. II. 18. No. 2, a. o.).[11] "Ius" has an ethical implication like the law, because "ius is precisely the same as that which is just, and just is in turn, precisely the equitable and the good" (DL. I. 2 No. 4).[12]

1.3 Natural law. "Natural law" (DL. II. 5 - 16) is the first system "whereby the eternal law has been applied or made known to us, in a twofold way, first through natural reason, and secondly through the laws of the Decalogue written on the Mosaic tablets."[13] Natural law consists of an inherent obligation to the intrinsically good, never allowing any bad. It includes also an inherent sanction, seeking an enforceable obligation. It is not a constitution of law, but a declaration of law; that is, it does not create good or bad but indicates actions that are good or bad. It

---

11. Scott, 159. Here we can find the "ius ad rem" and the "ius in re." Consequently Grotius in 1625 was not the first who rediscovered this threefold answer (De iure belli ac pacis I. I. II. 1), as Haggenmacher asserts (1983,462). Suárez himself developed this answer in 1613.

12. Scott, 136.

13. DL. Second book. Foreword; for the following: Scott, 138, 142f., 153 and 155f.

binds conscience by reason itself and is recognisable by natural illumination as well as by one or more discursive reflections. It presents itself in prohibitions, precepts in the narrow sense, permissions, or concessions (cf. DL. II. 6, II. 9, II. 14 and II. 18. No. 2).

Natural law in Suárez' view is, first, always just because it is equipped with the "nuances" necessary to regulate any case in all its peculiarities. It is aware of the specificity of the case to be treated. It has complete respect for circumstances and conditions. The question arises whether the determination of circumstances under which laws are not binding is a matter of equity (aequitas). But the famous "necessity knows no law" − "necessitas non habet legem" − has no significance at all in the Suárezian system of law. Each necessity is foreseen by the law and regulated. Legitimate self-defence is not outside the law, but permitted by it. And consequently the natural law precept is equitable in itself; it does not admit any kind of equity, in the sense of correction and amelioration of the law.

Second, natural law does not provide a clear scale of fines or punishments; it is only an assessing law.

Third, natural law is unaffected by any changes in the human world of norms, contracts, or laws − as little as God is affected by any changes in the world. When a contract is fulfilled, the norm "pacta sunt servanda" remains unchanged and in place. And when a human law gets abrogated, the norm of the natural law remains in force. Change and abolition in human legal affairs imply no change in the norm of the natural law.

Fourth, Suárez is very interested in the relation seen in the natural law between the realms of God and man, grace and nature, reason and will, general and special, and also universal and particular. One example can serve to illustrate more clearly how the natural law stands in relation to specific cases of human lawmaking: A political community needs to be invented. Once it is established with its human laws, the natural law demands obedience to the laws. If there are contracts or conventions or pacts, they are the result of free human activity; once they are established, the natural law demands obedience because of the moral principle "pacta sunt servanda" (DL II. 13. No. 7 - 9, II. 14. No. 11, II. 17. No. 9, II. 19. No. 7 and III. 3. No. 2 and 6).

1.4 The human or civil law. The civil law, the law of the nation state (DL. III. 1 - 4; especially III. 4. No. 7), is (in contrast to the natural law) human and not divine, artificial and not natural, external and not inherent, constitutive and not declarative. Civil law is mutable and allows the application of equity to correct these imperfections. The force and efficacy of human law comes directly from the will of the human legislator.[14]

1.5 The law of nations. This law, for which Suárez uses the term "ius gentium," is of all man-made systems the most closely related to the natural law (DL. II. 17. No. 7; II. 19. No. 3).[15] Indeed, the content of the ius gentium is partly natural law, more exactly the law that all human beings have in their common human nature, a law that human beings inherit and do not make. But we find also additions to this core made from time to time on the initiative of a state or a number of states, to meet their special needs – additions like agreements among states (DL. II. 17. No. 8 and II. 19. No. 3). This gives us two meanings of ius gentium, each understood in a twofold way.

1) The ius gentium is for Suárez a law in the strictly legal

---

14. DL. III foreword and III. 4. No. 1; Scott, 140.

15. For the following cf. Scott, 138, 157 and 185.

sense of the word (DL. II. 17. No. 2); but there are, as he has already observed (see 1.2 above), two kinds of laws, lex and ius (DL. II 19. No. 8). And as ius is the concomitant of gentium - indeed is that upon which 'gentium' depends - it is essential to make the choice. Finally Suárez prefers to speak of the ius gentium as lex.

2) We have to distinguish also between ius <u>inter</u> gentes and ius <u>intra</u> gentem or gentes (DL. II. 19. No. 8 and II. 20. 1., No. 6 and 8): "In the Roman law, which Suárez knew so well, and in the parlance of the jurists, of the canonists, and of the theologians, the term ius gentium was used in a twofold sense; or, as Suárez puts it, was viewed in two different aspects: <u>first</u>, as the Law which all the various peoples and nations ought to observe in their relations with each other ["ius inter gentes"]." - <u>Secondly</u>: "as a body of laws which individual states [...] observe within their own borders, but which is called ius gentium because these laws are similar (in each instance) and are commonly accepted" [ius intra gentem or gentes].[16] The concept of "ius inter gentes" did not prevail against the "ius gentium."

a) Concerning the <u>first</u> type, law governing relations between peoples and nations – laws "introduced simply through usage and tradition by means of [...] propagation and mutual imitation among the nations, rather than of pact and agreement among nations" (DL. II. 19. No. 6 and 9, II. 20. 1. No. 1 and III. 2. No. 6) – two remarks are necessary. First, I would like to call attention to the words "propagation" and "imitation" in the quotation above. Many examples confirm these two processes. There is, of course, the active expansion of constitutional elements by such processes as amendment. But there is also pure and simple mime-

---

16. Scott, 178.

sis, such as the copying of treaties of extradition, of solutions for asylum cases, and so forth. Lawyers and historians of the law of nations, in enumerating the many factors creating the law of nations, usually give pride of place to formal pacts among nations; but this is not the case for Suárez. For him customs and habits are much more decisive than agreements in developing the law of nations, notwithstanding that he knows both sources very well, custom and contract. Second, in this connection it is worth noting that building an international community seems to be taking place by an unplanned process. "The growing of the international community can be considered as a well-nigh natural process."[17]

b) As for the second type, law observed within a state (DL. II. 19. No. 6 and 10): It involves certain precepts, particular usages, or modes of living together, which are not in themselves and directly fitted for all humankind (as are the principles of international law proper). Neither do they have for their immediate end, so to speak, the harmonious fellowship and respectful intercourse of all nations.[18] This law is administered in each state by its own courts, according to appropriate rules. "The content is not derived from natural law, but it is so closely related to the human nature and is so thoroughly in accord or harmony with nature that through it the individual nations could easily have been led to adopt the rules in question."[19]

There are differences in how changes can take place in these two kinds of laws. The "ius intra gentem," according to Suárez, is intrinsically nothing more or less than civil law and can be changed by an individual state, at its will, but only to an extent

---

17. DL. II. 19. No.6; Scott, 185.

18. DL. II. 20. No. 10; Scott, 178.

19. DL. II. 19. No. 10 and II. 20. No.1; Scott, 186.

affecting that state alone (DL. II. 20. No. 7). And the ius inter gentes? Changes are far more difficult, because this law is introduced by the authority of all the states, so it may not be annulled without universal consent. But a change in the ius gentium would not be inconsistent with reason. Certainly, all nations should agree to an alteration if, for example, a custom contrary to some established rule of the ius gentium should gradually come into practice and prevail (DL. II. 20. No. 6 and 8).[20]

2. The Possibility of Particularity and of Universality

2.1 Particularity. Suárez follows the political thinking of Aristotle. I would like to discuss two theses basically taken from Aristotle and developed by Suárez.

The first Aristotelian thesis: The institution of civil magistrates endowed with the power of ruling over men is just and thoroughly in accord with human nature. Suárez offers two explications of this thesis, along the following lines.

First, man is a social animal and cherishes a natural, right desire to live in a community (DL. I. 6. No. 19 - 22; III. 1. No. 3). There are two types of communities, one imperfect, for example the family, the other perfect, the polis, the state. All these communities are limited with regard to persons, relations, territory, and aims. Human social life as such is limited life, never unlimited. What I have already explored above in the context of natural law needs only to be specified briefly here: Persons live together out of their free will; and as soon as they form a "collectio," the right and duty to shape the frame they have voluntarily chosen arise immedi-

---

20. Scott, 190-192.

ately without any further act by anyone. However, this frame obliges them to establish a government – a supreme authority, a judiciary, a legislative and an executive body, and so forth. The first step is voluntary, but it leads directly to obligations that bind even if not affirmed voluntarily and that cannot be modelled on principle. Governments, in turn, are subject to the obligation to provide the bonum commune. In this respect they also are not free. Their freedom lies, rather, in deciding the type of institutions they want to establish and in choosing how to establish them. These thoughts of Suárez can help us in our effort to rethink the state.

Suárez' second explication starts from the premise that in a perfect community there must be a power in charge of governing the community (DL. III. 1. No. 4 and 5). This power is sole, unique, and indivisible; but as human political power, it is also necessarily limited. There are always geographical borders, boundaries, and frontiers. And boundaries between states are normative as well as physical; for instance, laws demanding obedience, liberties demanding respect. Suárez writes in this chapter: "Outside of his own territory he who declares a law may be disobeyed with impunity." No law may exceed the limits of the jurisdiction of the one who enacts it. Suárez underlines the affirmation by the word of St. Paul: 'Now we are well aware, that whatever the Law says is said for those who are subject to the Law'.[21] The competence of the lawgiver ends at the limits of his district, and if he goes beyond his competence and makes laws for people living outside, this people can refuse obedience. Punishment for disobedience in such a case would be illegal and illegitimate.[22] However, humankind does not form an integrated community

---

21. Romans 3, 19; Dig. II. 1. 20.

22. Liber Sextus. I. 2. 2; Scott, 135.

without borders, and thus there will be persons living outside the governing power of any given nation state. Consequently, there is almost infinite opportunity for legitimate and lawful disobedience; that is, among persons who belong to no particular state.

Suárez mentioned several times a ban on crossing borders. His interest might be easier for us to understand when we realize that he thought implicitly of a law for mankind that recognizes no territorial impediments but has an all-inclusive jurisdiction. However, it is impossible that Suárez meant by this the natural law: although the natural law does apply universally to every person and excludes no one, still it lacks an external, binding form.

The second Aristotelian thesis: A human magistrate, if supreme in his or her own order, has the power, the right and the obligation to make laws suitable for that particular sphere. Whoever has power, bears responsibility. A supreme position involves obligations (DL III. 1. No. 6 and 7).

Taken together, these two theses express the basic structure, and explain the grounds for the legitimacy, of power. Now the result: At all levels of the constitution of a community (except the constitution of the family) – of a government, of elections, and so forth – we can remark that an element of consensus is necessary, constitutive, and active (DL. III. 2. No. 2, 4 and 5; III. 3. No. 1 and III. 4. No. 2). Consensus, not a contract. A contract is concluded between the bottom and the top level, but always between persons, between the people and their ruler. For Suárez, in contrast, consensus is the way to enter a meaningful construction made by God; consensus represents the fulfilment of a given plan. In "De opere sex dierum" Suárez speaks apparently of a contract: "Alius ergo modus multiplicationis familiarum seu domorum est cum distinctione domestica et aliqua unione politica, quae non fit sine aliquo pacto expresso vel tacito iuvandi se invicem, nec sine aliqua subordinatione familiarum et personarum ad aliquem superiorem vel rectorem communitatis sine quo talis communitas constare non potest."[23] In DL, though, he abandoned this line of argument. There he speaks about the establishment of society through nature and about the obligation of the people to seek an accord, a consensus with the will of God (DL. I. 7. No. 4, I. 11. No. 4 and 7, III. 2. No. 3 and III. 3. 1).

2.2 Universality. Suárez discusses also in this regard what is matter of fact. Pluralism exists, and human beings have never been able to surmount it; it has not been possible to found a world state.

But Suárez also says, and his view is surely not superficial: "The rational basis of this branch of law [the ius gentium], indeed, consists in the fact that the human race, howsoever many the various peoples . . . into which it may be divided, always preserves a certain unity not only as a species, but also, as it were, a moral and political unity called for by the natural precept of mutual love and mercy, which applies to all, even to strangers of any nation" (DL. II. 19. No. 9). "Moral and political unity"? Does this justify talking about the idea of a universal community as a juridical person bound by a law?[24]

"Therefore although a given sovereign state [. . .] may constitute a perfect community in itself, consisting of its own members, nevertheless, each one of these states is also, in a certain sense, and viewed in relation to the human race, a member of that universal society; for never are these states, when standing alone, so self-sufficient that they do not require some mutual assistance,

---

23. De opere sex dierum. Lib. V. Cap. 7, in: Vivès, Vol. 3 [Paris 1856] 413-419 [414].

24. Soder 1965, 15; Scott 181f.

association and intercourse, at times for their greater welfare and advantage, but at other times because also of some moral necessity or lack, as is clear from experience."²⁵ Soder draws our attention to the fact that for Suárez, sovereignty of states is compatible with international jurisdiction (cf. "Defensio fidei". Lib. IV. Cap. 7. No. 6).

How does a government justify itself? Through its achievements: the results of its work are the primary justification for a government. Achievements, however, are not just any activities by that government but only successful policies for the common good.

2.3 Problems of a global state. Suárez discusses the question of a global state at various points in his works. He remarks, that this political power today does not exist in the way of one, unique power for mankind. There is no competent power for the convention of all the men living in the world today because there are no conventions of this universal kind (DL. III. 2. No. 5 and III. 4. No. 7). Having proved that a global state is as a matter of fact impossible, Suárez adduces three normative arguments to show that a global state is undesirable.

The argument from illegitimacy: Legitimacy in a strict and formal sense is conferred by an assembly of persons who will be affected by a future governing power. A world government presupposes a world community because, first, only such a community can transfer the power of political organisation to a government and, second, only such a community can establish the form of its polity. But in reality it would be impossible to convene such an assembly or to bring about such a vote. Therefore, there is a

---

25. DL. II. 19. No. 9; Scott, 182.

danger that anyone striving to erect a world government would be aiming consciously at founding an illegitimate entity (DL. III. 4. No. 7).

The argument from lack of necessity: A world state is unneeded as long as a variety of states can achieve the global common good. A global state would be desirable only if it could provide a higher level of comprehensive happiness than some interrelated plurality of states. In contrast, if the consequences of world government were to include standardisation, a decline of challenges or healthy competition, or even limitation of them, then such a state would have to be rejected on moral grounds. (cf. "De triplici virtute". Tract. I. Disp. 9. S. 6. No. 17 and DL. III. 2. No. 5.) Suárez did not believe a world-wide government necessary to keep humankind in a good condition.

The argument from inability to govern: Although it has up to today been impossible to bring all people in the world together, should this be desired? Suárez declared, No! Aristotle[26] said that a "civitas" or "polis" becomes very difficult to govern above a relatively small population. It would be even more difficult to deal with a "regnum" and impossible to put together a competent global government (DL. III. 2. No. 5 and "De bello". Sect. 6. No. 6).[27]

2.4 International law. However, despite the drawbacks of world government as such, there remains a need for law at the level of international relations: "Consequently, such communities have need of some system of law, whereby they may be directed and properly ordered with regard to this kind of intercourse and association; and although this law is in large measure provided by

---

26. Aristotle. Pol. Lib. VI. Chapt. 4 (1291a 40 - 1291b 1); Scott 249f.

27. Soder 1965, 16. Anm. 34; Scott 249f.

natural reason, it is not provided in sufficient measure and in a direct manner, with respect to all matters. Therefore it was possible for certain special rules of law to be introduced through the practice of these same nations" (DL. II. 19. No. 9).

"For just as in one society or province law is introduced by custom; so among the human race as a whole it was possible for laws to be introduced by the habitual conduct of nations, and all the more because the matters comprised within this latter system of law are few, and very closely related to the natural law, and most easily deduced therefrom in a manner so advantageous and so in harmony with nature itself, that while this derivation of the ius gentium from the natural law, may not be self-evident, that is, not essentially and absolutely required for moral rectitude, it is nevertheless quite in accord with nature, and universally acceptable for its own sake" (DL. II. 19. No. 9).[28]

3. The International Community

The equality of all states flows from the premise that the "consensus" creating each of them is made by human beings, all of whom are themselves equal. Men and women join in a political community and erect a political structure for themselves; in this respect, all political communities are equal. Where would a qualitative difference among political communities come from? Therefore, when looking – in the Aristotelian language congenial to Suárez – to the efficient cause (causa efficiens), all states are equal, regardless of religion or military power. And when considering the final cause (causa finalis), a state is a state if it has a territory and a

---

28. Scott, 182f.

people and it accepts the obligation to procure the welfare of the population (DL. II. 19). Suárez argues for a normative concept of the state: The state is only a state, a "res publica," if it endeavours to provide for the common good of all.

"The international community is by the very existence of states an organic community, with the power to make laws to prevent the violation of the obligation, which every state has by reason of its existence and membership in the community." "Violation is an offense not merely against the nation involved, but against all nations, as all are bound by and are beneficiaries under the natural law: it is a right of every nation to insist that the ius gentium should be respected and that therefore the obligation under ius gentium, which pertains to the natural law, should be observed in its entirety." This argument provides the pope with a legal basis for intervention in the name of defending the natural law.

"Now an obligation on the part of one nation creates a right on the part of another, and the right, like the obligation, from which it flows, is under the protection of the natural law." "If the rights of one nation under natural law can be violated, the rights of all nations under natural law are endangered."[29]

4. Mediation between Universality and Particularities

The forerunners and models for mediation between the universal and the particular lie, for Suárez, in the realm of personal and social activities in a rather narrow sense. Whoever does

---

29. Scott, 181 und 185.

something good to himself, does it to himself as a person and not only to a particular part of his body. Whoever takes care of himself in a morally good way – and inevitably he also takes care of himself as a member of a political community – takes care of a morally good concern of the political community insofar as the political community is based on and nourished by the economy, culture, religion, and so forth. Hence we can say that, whenever a civitas, a regnum, an imperium, and also the Church takes care of itself, it strengthens and fosters the common life of the human race (the collectio hominum universalis).

The relation between universalism and particularism cannot be determined in a plan made in advance or by way of a political calculation. Suárez gives in this context ample space to habits ("consuetudo"), to the customs that develop at the basis of society, to the "usus," and to an implicitly accepted proceeding by way of trial and error – something he seems to regard as unnecessary for intra-state life.

For Suárez, there existed "una societas humana" – something like a generic human "background society" – on the basis of which a specifically Christian society (societas christiana) developed (DL. III. 2. No. 6). The societas christiana was able to establish its particular laws, as in the case of Christian soldiers captured in war: Christendom had abolished the right of the victorious (Christian) party to enslave defeated soldiers if they were Christian. We would still have to determine whether Suàrez was here thinking specifically about the problem of particularities. At least he was thinking of fairness and equity, which softens the rigid application of a principle and adjusts it to the circumstances. He voiced the principle "Salus animarum suprema lex" that, in my view, also was directed to the individual person rather than a particular culture. In reality, most representatives of the Church thought in "Western," "European" terms, not in more global categories. Although the popes favoured Portugal, Spain, and the Catholic countries over the Protestant countries, they nevertheless kept to generically European formulae, ideas, and habits. To apply equity world-wide was not difficult in principle but still a real challenge in practice.

Appendix:

In one of his texts Suárez writes about "accomoda partitio" (DL. III. 4. No. 7). This can be interpreted to mean that peoples spread, expand, or retreat, or at least they demarcate borders and respect them, and a state of wholesome distribution is reached. Propaganda like "Volk ohne Raum" ("a people without space"), and likewise talk about some people living in the servants' quarters while others live in the manor house, or again, thinking in terms of security interests does not have an echo nor find any support in such calm and sensible language. It should be clear by now that Suàrez' view amounts to wishful thinking.

References

Brouillard, René, "Francisco Suárez," Section 4: "Théologie politique," in Dictionnaire de théologie catholique, vol. 14, part 2 (Paris, 1941), col. 2709-78.

Haggenmacher, Peter, Grotius et la doctrine de la guerre juste (Paris, 1983).

Mesnard, Pierre, L'essor de la philosophie politique au XVIe siècle

(Paris, 1936).

Rommen, Hans, Die Staatslehre des F. Suárez (Mönchen-Gladbach, 1926).

Schuster, Johann Baptist SJ, "Die Lehre des Franz Suárez über den ursprünglichen Träger der Staatsgewalt und ihre Kritik durch Viktor Cathrein," Scholastik 16 (1941): 379-87.

Scott, James Brown, The Catholic Conception of International Law: Francisco de Vitoria, Founder of the Modern Law of Nations; Francisco Suárez, Founder of the Modern Philosophy of Law in General and in Particular of the Law of Nations: A Critical Examination and a Justified Appreciation (Washington D.C., 1934).

Soder, Hans, "Franz Suárez und sein Werk," Introduction to Francisco Suárez: Ausgewählte Texte ("Die Klassiker des Völkerrechts," vol. 4), ed. Josef de Vries SJ (Tübingen, 1965), pp. 1-19.

Soder, Hans, Francisco Suárez und das Völkerrecht: Grundgedanken zu Staat, Recht und internationalen Beziehungen (Frankfurt am Main, 1973).

Suárez, Francisco SJ, Opera Omnia [Vivès edition], 28 vols. (Paris, 1856-1878).

Suárez, Francisco, De legibus, ed. Luciano Pereña et al. De legibus ac Deo legislatore [unfinished critical edition, Latin and Spanish] ("Corpus Hispanorum de Pace" [CHP], vol. 11-17 and 21-22; Madrid, 1971ff.). (I cited De legibus, Foreword, I.1-I.8 = CHP XI [Madrid, 1971]; De legibus, I.9-I.20 = CHP XII [Madrid, 1972]; De legibus, Foreword, II.1-II.12 = CHP XIII [Madrid, 1974]; De legibus, II.13-II.20 = CHP XIV [Madrid, 1973]; De legibus, Foreword, III.1-III.16 = CHP XV [Madrid, 1975].)

Peace through a Public Global Authority in Papal Teaching from Leo XIII to John XXIII

Heinz-Gerhard Justenhoven

Peoples and nations made their second attempt in the twentieth century to overcome war permanently when the United Nations was founded. In future, individual states should not be allowed to use war as a means of achieving political goals. Until the beginning of the First World War, the right to wage war was not only common practice, but also permitted under international law. This right to wage war, which had been a matter of course for every sovereign state since the beginning of the modern era, was now to be prohibited under international law. The question of how this prohibition of war can be secured institutionally and how it can be implemented in an emergency is still being argued about today. Only when all the members of the community of nations can rely on every other nation observing the prohibition of war - either voluntarily or by force - will anarchy between nations be overcome.

The contribution of Christians to this discussion was given new impetus in 1894 when Pope Leo XIII addressed all the princes and peoples of the earth with his peace encyclical "Praeclara gratulationis." Now it was not only individual Christians or initiatives striving for peace between the nations; the Pope himself, as head of the Catholic Church, made this his special cause. He did not want to limit himself solely to particular initiatives, he wanted to lay the theoretical foundation for an international system from the perspective of Christian belief. And church teaching today is still following the example set by Pope Leo XIII. The popes therefore actively participate in the search for a way to overcome war permanently. The question is whether a peace system should be based on the system of sovereign states or whether a new international order is required which removes power from the sovereign state.

Church teaching does not see the answer to the question of how war can be permanently overcome in maintaining, unaltered, the present system of sovereign states. What is needed, as the Second Vatican Council concluded in 1965, is "a universal public authority, recognized by all, which will possess the effective means on behalf of all to safeguard security, the observance of justice and respect for rights."[1] With this statement, church teaching goes far beyond the United Nations Charter. There it is stated that the United Nations is based on the principle of the sovereign equality of all its members (Art. 2). On the one hand the United Nations Charter has prohibited violence by international law and thereby limited the sovereignty of the member states, but on the other it has made no provision for the institutional implementation of this prohibition. The demand for a universal public authority, as developed in papal teachings from Leo XIII (1894) to John XXIII (1963) will be discussed below.

Translated by Dr. Madeleine Resuehr, Hamburg

1. Second Vatican Council, "Pastoral Constitution on the Church in the World of Today," 82, in Decrees of the Ecumenical Councils, ed. Norman P. Tanner (London and Washington, 1990) 2: 1128.

1. Leo XIII: International Law Based on Natural Law

Leo XIII, on St. Peter's chair from 1878-1903, was the first pope after the loss of the Papal States under his predecessor, Pius IX. The secular influence which had sprung from political sovereignty diminished as a result. Under Pope Leo XIII the Church turned its attention to the moral problems of the modern world, going through the process of industrialization. Leo's main concerns in view of the state of the world at the time were the social situation of workers and the gigantic rearmament programs. These programs were using up enormous financial and moral resources, which, as a result, were then not available to alleviate social problems.

The Vatican Secretary of State Cardinal Rampolla stated in 1898 that the rearmament at the end of the nineteenth century was the result of a lack of an international legal order. Rampolla wrote, "What the international community of nations lacks is a system of legal and moral means which could determine and make valid the rights of each individual. As a result, there is no choice but direct recourse to violence, and this, in turn, is the reason for the competition between the nations to develop their military power.[2]

It is therefore not surprising that Leo XIII expressly supported Tsar Nicolas I in 1898 when he called a peace conference. The fact that Leo felt entitled to be an arbitrator in political matters, however, needed explanation. "How could the advocacy (*advocatio*) of the Pope be of more value," Leo wrote, than "in the effort to secure peace between the nations and in reducing both the

---

2. Second reply from Secretary of State Cardinal Rampolla to the second Russian circular regarding the Hague Peace Conference, quoted from Hans Wehberg, Das Papsttum und der Weltfriede (Mönchengladbach, 1915), 99 (German text).

frequency and horror of wars? For the task God Himself has set the Papacy is to stand for justice, bring about peace, prevent conflict."[3] There was a program behind Pope Leo's claim. Leo still understood the papacy as holding universal power over the particular interests of individual states. In 1899 he wrote to the Dutch Queen Wilhelmina, "Indeed, the power of the pontifical office does not stop at national borders; it includes all peoples, in order to unite them in the true peace of the Gospel. The involvement of this office in the advancement of the general well-being of humankind raises it above the particular interests of heads of state, and no-one is in a better position to restore harmony between so many spiritually different peoples."[4]

According to Oskar Köhler, comparing Leo with the medieval Pope Innocent III, whom Leo greatly admired, makes it easier to understand the later pope's concept of papal authority over political power. Like his great predecessor, Leo wanted to "establish a papacy which, in the post-revolutionary world, once again and adjusted accordingly, takes up the universal historical mission which it had fulfilled in the Middle Ages, and wins back 'moral religious hegemony in a new Christian universal empire.'"[5]

The international community needed "a system of legal and moral means which could determine and make valid the rights of each individual,"[6] wrote Secretary of State Cardinal Rampolla in

---

3. Leo XIII, Allocutio "Auspicandae celebritatis," in: Acta Sancta Sedis (hereafter ASS) 32, 1899-1900, 322 (Latin original).

4. Epistolam quam Leo Papa XIII ad Wilhelminam Hollandiae Reginam rescribens misit (29.5.1899), in: ASS 32, 1899-1900, 66 (French original).

5. Oskar Köhler, "Der Weltplan Leos XIII.: Ziele und Methoden," in: Handbuch der Kirchengeschichte, vol. 6, part 2, ed. Hubert Jedin (Freiburg u. a., 1985), 21f (German text).

6. Second reply from Secretary of State Cardinal Rampolla, quoted from

1898 before the Hague Peace Conference began. Peace could only be permanent if "based on public Christian law." On this rested "the concord between the princes themselves and the concord between the nations and their princes." The public Christian law which Leo's spokesman refers to here bears similarities to the public law of late Spanish scholasticism, which was based on natural law and which bound states both internally and externally.[7] The Pope therefore objects to "understanding contemporary law as meaning that relations between the nations must be regulated by a new legal system based on the principle of usefulness, on the prevalence of violence, on the success of *faits accomplis* and on other factors which are a negation of the eternal and unalterable principles of justice."[8] The classical public international law of the nineteenth century was a long way from its origins, its natural law foundations, and therefore from its firm connection to justice. In the era of the absolute sovereignty of national states, it had degenerated to a law of the *fait accompli*, a law, therefore, which accepted the normativity of whatever situation existed.

The result, according to Leo XIII, is that "there has risen little by little, in the international order, a system of jealous egoism, in consequence of which the nations now watch each other, if not with hate, at least with the suspicion of rivals. Hence, in their great undertaking they lose sight of the lofty principles of morality and

---

Wehberg, 99.

7. See Heinz-Gerhard Justenhoven, Francisco de Vitoria zu Krieg und Frieden (Köln, 1990), 64f; Francisco de Vitoria, Vorlesungen I-II. Völkerrecht-Politik-Kirche (Latin-German edition) ed. U. Horst, H. G. Justenhoven, and J. Stüben (Stuttgart, 1995-97).

8. First reply from Secretary of State Cardinal Rampolla of 15 September 1898 to the Russian circular regarding the Hague Peace Conference, quoted from Wehberg, 97f.

justice and forget the protection which the feeble and oppressed have a right to demand. In the desire . . . to increase their riches, they regard only the opportunity which circumstances afford, the advantages of successful enterprises, and the tempting bait of an accomplished fact, sure that no-one will trouble them in the name of right or the respect which right can claim. Such are the fatal principles which have consecrated material power as the supreme law of the world . . . ."[9] This unbridled egoism of the states, contained only by the limits of their power, "is to be imputed [to] the limitless increase of military establishments and that armed peace which in many respects is equivalent to a disastrous war."[10]

Let us summarize church teaching on peace under Leo XIII at the end of the nineteenth century: Pope Leo criticized the then current popular concept of international law which sanctioned the right of the stronger. This way of thinking led, in his opinion, to the gigantic build-up of arms which in fact exploded in the First World War eleven years after his death. Leo believed the arms race could be prevented if the medieval ideal of concord among the princes under the pope on the basis of a common law, international law based on natural law, was restored.[11] In the role of an arbitrator, Leo wanted to issue legally binding judgments, based on this international law, on the disputes of the princes and thus serve peace between the nations. Even though Leo's suggestions did not meet with success during his life, he did create the framework

---

9. Leo XIII, Letter "Pervenuti," 19 March 1902, in: Principles for Peace: Selections from Papal Documents, ed. Harry C. Koenig (Washington, 1943), 107.

10. Ibid.

11. Cf. Leo XIII Praeclara gratulationis, 20 June 1894, in: ASS 26, 1893-94, 714 f (Latin original).

which the popes of the twentieth century elaborated and changed in their own thinking about peace.

2. Benedict XV: United Nations with Effective International Arbitration

Benedict XV was elected Pope in 1914, shortly after the outbreak of the First World War. He was forced to state his position immediately: of the 300 million Catholics in the world at the time, 190 million were involved in the war - 124 million on the side of the entente, 64 million on the side of the Central Powers.[12] Pope Benedict delivered many speeches on the basic principles of peace and attempted to mediate discreetly on many occasions in order to bring about an end to the war. His last public appeal for peace on 1 August 1917 is famous.[13] As a young monsignor, Benedict XV had worked in the State Secretariat under Leo XIII and was a close friend of Secretary of State Rampolla. He knew Leo's thinking and linked his own with it.

The "nations are naturally bound to each other by mutual dependence like mutual good will."[14] Benedict regarded this unity as not simply functional, but as based on the theology of creation. Even if war does not destroy this interdependence, it certainly

---

12. Cf. Konrad Repgen, "Papsttum und Staatenkonflikte im 20. Jahrhundert," in: Dieter Oberndörfer and Karl Schmitt, eds., Kirche und Demokratie (Paderborn, 1983), 156.

13. Cf. Benedict XV, "From the Beginning: The Pope's Peace Appeal to Heads of Belligerent Nations," American Journal of International Law, Supplement 11, 1917, 212-215; hereafter cited as Benedict XV, "From the Beginning."

14. Cf. Benedict XV, Pacem dei, in: Acta Apostolicae Sedis (hereafter cited as AAS) XII, 1920, 215 (Latin original).

endangers its very foundations. In order to be protected against war in the future, Benedict suggested a "union of the nations" (*consociatio gentium*) "to protect the freedom of each and every individual and to preserve the order of human society."[15] These "united nations" (*nationes foederates*) could model themselves on the church as the "perfect original universal society" (*ecclesia, quae cum absolutissimum sit societatis universalis exemplar*) with regard both to the principle of order and to institutions, since the church was also able to bring people together in temporal matters. Benedict lent weight to this argument by referring to the historical achievements of the church in the formation of a Christian Europe during the Middle Ages.

The community of nations proposed by Benedict was to be based on "the moral force of right," which was to replace "the material force of arms."[16] Benedict did not develop an understanding of international law, but referred only to the fact that states too must recognize the dignity of human beings.[17] In future, conflict between nations should be settled by a court of arbitration instead of by armies.[18] Pope Benedict was aware that the first Hague Peace Conference in 1899 had agreed on a voluntary arbitration procedure between states. Unlike the arbitration court already in existence, however, Benedict, like Leo XIII, insisted on "safeguarding against any state which should refuse to submit to the court of arbitration or to accept decisions made on international questions."[19] The sovereignty of states is limited in two ways by

---

15. Cf. Benedict XV, Pacem dei, in: AAS XII, 1920, 216.

16. Benedict XV, "From the Beginning," 212.

17. Cf. Benedict XV, Ad beatissimi, in: AAS VI, 1914, 568f (Latin original).

18. Cf. Benedict XV, "From the Beginning," 214 f.

19. Ibid.

this demand for obligatory arbitration. First, Benedict demands that states give up the right to wage war without juridical limitation; states would in future be obliged to take all questions of conflict to the court of arbitration. The usual use of arms to gain real or imagined right, which had hitherto prevailed, would be denied them. And second, the states were to accept an authority which would decide the dispute, independently of the will of the states involved, and which would enforce its decision. After all, Benedict demands safeguards against any state refusing to accept the decision of the court of arbitration. Still, he gives no indication of how the community of nations was to enforce this law.

In 1899 Pope Leo had made it clear to Queen Wilhelmina that he was reclaiming the role of arbitrator in disputes between nations because of what he understood to be his pontifical office. The will of the powers frustrated this undertaking. What did Benedict XV learn from Leo's experience? Pope Benedict saw himself as the "interpreter and keeper of eternal law" (*interpres et vindex legis aeternae*).[20] He preaches the "law of the love of the Gospel" (*evangelica lex caritatis*), which is "valid in the same way both for individuals and for states and nations."[21] Therefore Benedict sees it as "one of the most important duties of the pope to explain that nobody, for any reason, may ever violate justice." This, he told the College of Cardinals in 1915, "we declare candidly and freely and condemn all violations of the law most strongly, wherever they may occur."[22]

---

20. Benedict XV, Allocutio habita in consistorio diei 22 Ianuarii, in: AAS VII, 1915, 34 (Latin original).

21. Benedict XV, Pacem dei 16, in: AAS XII, 1920, 215.

22. Benedict XV, Allocutio habita in consistorio diei 22 Ianuarii, in: AAS VII, 1915, 34.

Did Benedict want to intervene directly in the conflicts between states? It almost seems so, when he says of himself, "We have, so to say, thrown Ourselves into the midst of the warring nations as a father throws himself into the disputes of his children . . . they swore to forego their plans to destroy each other . . . . Unfortunately Our fatherly warning has not been heeded to this day, and war, with all its horrors, continues to rage."[23] Benedict could only watch while the states "opposed his pleas" and "his repeated appeal for peace did not meet with the desired success."[24] In this, his experience was similar to Leo XIII's; he found out that although he can call for an end to conflict, he does not have the means to bring it about and the states do not grant him these means.

Consequently, obligatory arbitration cannot be forced on the states; they must agree to accept it and support it. The court of arbitration which was to be set up should, wrote Benedict, become active according to "rules to be drawn in concert."[25] Here Benedict drew the obvious conclusions from the powers' objection, even during peacetime, to Leo's desire to reclaim the papal office of arbitrator. The powers were willing to accept neither obligatory arbitration nor the pope as arbitrator. The pope could only remind them of the ethical principles of peace and urge them to implement them soon.

---

23. Benedict XV, Al tremendo conflitto, in: AAS 1916, 58f (Italian original).

24. Ibid.

25. Cf. Benedict XV, "From the Beginning," 214f.

3. Pius XII: Relative Sovereignty of States and Effective International Authority

Pius XII was elected pope on 2 March 1939, just a few months before the Second World War started. During the war he stated his position on basic questions of international order again and again. Among his most important messages were his Christmas radio broadcasts. Pius XII developed Pope Benedict's thinking further, giving it a natural law foundation.[26] In order to achieve peaceful coexistence of nations and overcome war, the nations must, in the pope's opinion, "act according to the plan drawn up by nature." "The most important guidelines come from a clear knowledge and observation of the nature of human beings, the nature of things and the resultant relationships and requirements."[27] In his broad natural law system, Pius XII begins by assuming the will of the Creator to be the highest law that man can recognize and according to which he must organize his national and international community in order to find peace.

God is the source of all order, which is expressed in eternal law. Eternal law functions in the intrinsic characteristic order of all things.[28] In the "area of conscious human activity, . . . the ordering will of the Creator manifests itself by way of the moral command-

---

26. My research on Pius XII has benefited from the German edition, Aufbau und Entfaltung des gesellschaftlichen Lebens. Soziale Summe Pius XII., ed. A. Utz and J. Groner (Freiburg, Switzerland, 1954-1961).

27. Pius XII, Allocutiones dirigentibus ac Sociis Sodalitatis Italicae, in: AAS XLVII, 1955, 770 (Italian original).

28. Cf. Pius XII, Nuntius Radiophonicus 24.12.1957, in: AAS L, 1958, 5ff (Italian original).

ment of God, as it is set out in nature and in Revelation."[29] Man fulfills the moral demands placed upon him if he keeps God's commandment, which is recognizable by reason. "If man keeps to and acts according to these norms, his actions will naturally be in harmony with the general order desired by the Creator."[30] "What the nations so strongly desire after the trials and ruins of this war in the way of a new order," the Pope said in 1941 in the middle of the world war, "must be based on the unshakeable foundations of the moral law which the Creator Himself laid down through the order of nature and which is written indelibly in the hearts of humankind."[31]

3.1. Protection of Human Rights as the Goal of Social Order

Pius describes the human community as a very imperfect image of the Trinity, in the general sense of a system emanating from God and reflected in the world and society.[32] As an "image of the Trinity which redeemed and raised humankind by becoming man, the human community, in the light of reason and Revelation, possesses a moral authority and absolutism, both in its full meaning

---

29. Pius XII, Ad praelatos Auditores ceterosque Officiales et Administros Tribunalis Sacrae Romanae Rotae, in: AAS XLI, 1949, 606, (Italian original).
30. Ibid.
31. Pius XII, Nuntius Radiophonicus 24.12.1941, in: AAS XL, 1942, 16 (Italian original).
32. Cf. Joachim Giers, "Humanismus und christliche Ordnungsidee nach den Weihnachtsbotschaften Pius XII," in: H. Schambeck, ed., Pius XII. zum Gedächtnis (Berlin, 1977), 291.

and in its purpose, which survives the ebb and flow of time."[33] Joachim Giers interprets the words of Pius XII as meaning that "an absolute and essential order, which has its foundations in God, is required in the human community."[34] The aim of the life of the community is the "maintenance, development and perfection of the human personality. It should help each person to fulfill dutifully the religious and cultural tasks which the Creator has set the individual, the whole of humankind, and its natural divisions."

On this basis, Pius turns to the question of political order. The goal of all social life is the development of the personality of each human being in the image of God. In view of his experience of Fascist and Communist dictatorships, Pius sees democracy as the most just form of government. It is the nations themselves, he writes in his Christmas message in 1944, which have "taken on a new questioning, critical, distrustful attitude to the state and politicians. Because they have learned from bitter experience, they oppose most strongly the exclusive orders of a dictatorial, uncontrollable and untouchable power and demand a system of government which is more in harmony with the dignity and freedom of the citizens."[35] Democratic control of state power, as Pius summarizes the experiences of the nations, could have prevented the war. The nations "have become convinced . . . that the world would not have been drawn into the fateful turmoil of the war if it had been possible to examine and correct the activity of public power, and that it is necessary to create effective securities within the nations

---

33. Pius XII, Nuntius Radiophonicus 24.12.1942, in: AAS XXXV, 1943, 11 (Italian original).

34. J. Giers, 291.

35. The following quotations are from Pius XII, Nuntius Radiophonicus 24.12.1944, in: AAS XXXVII, 1945, 10-24 (Italian original).

in order to avoid a repetition of a similar catastrophe in the future." Pius sees this democratization as exclusively the task of the state. As a result, Pius sees the necessity of democratic control not only at the national level, but also at the level of the international institution. Therefore, "the democratic form of government appears to many to be the form dictated by reason." Pius sees democracy as the form of government under which the freedom of humankind can best be realized.

Basic human rights are "so inviolable as basic rights that no reasons of state, no pretense of what is for the common good may be brought to bear. They stand protected behind a barrier which cannot be overstepped. On this side of the barrier, laws can be passed for the common good as it pleases the people; but not beyond the barrier."[36] Pius justifies giving human rights priority over national legislation by stating that "human beings, by their very nature, were meant to live in society. However, as reason alone has taught us, society exists fundamentally for human beings, not human beings for society. Man received his right to his body and life not from society but from the Creator Himself, . . . It therefore follows that society cannot rob him directly of this right."[37] Human rights, according to Pius, are the right to worship God, the right to choose one's way of life, the right to choose one's profession freely, the right to private property, the right to emigrate, the right to impartial administration of the law, the right to work, and freedom of opinion.

A qualified legal order is necessary to protect basic rights. In 1942, Pius called for a rediscovery of "the consciousness of a

---

36. Pius XII, Ad philosophus studiis humanitatis, in: AAS XXXXI, 1949, 556 (French original).

37. Pius XII, Address to the Italian members of the Medical and Biological Union of St. Luke 12.11.1944, in: Utz and Groner, 2226 (German text).

legal order based on the supremacy of God and removed from any human arbitrariness, a legal order which holds its protective and vengeful hand over human rights which cannot be lost and removes them from the grasp of any human power."[38] The protection of human rights is the starting point not only for national but also for international order. Legal order serves community life "as an external support, as a screen and protection." It must "secure the balance between individuals and also between the divisions in the community and within these themselves." In order to secure the existence and the inner unity of the community, legal order "also has the power to act against those who can only be kept in the sublime law and order of community life in this way." Human beings need national order for their protection and development.

3.2. Fundamental Unity of Humankind as Basis of International Law

However, Pius reminds us at the same time that "the Catholic teaching of the state and bourgeois society . . . [was] always based on the principle that, according to God's will, all nations should form a community, with a common goal and common tasks."[39] Pius finds his reasons in the theology of creation: As "all men are the children of the one Father Who is in Heaven" and are predestined "to become true brothers,"[40] the "fate of peace"

---

38. The following quotations are from Pius XII, Nuntius Radiophonicus 24.12.1942.
39. Pius XII, Nuntius Radiophonicus 24.12.1948, in: AAS XXXXI, 1949, 10 (Italian original).
40. Pius XII, Letter to President Truman, 20 December 1949, in: Osservatore

depends on recognizing, as he stated in his Christmas message in 1944, "that the absolutely valid order of being and purpose, . . . as a moral requirement and the highest point of social development, also includes the unity of humankind and the family of nations."[41] Pius states as a requirement of the time that "sovereign states must . . . join to become a legal community."[42] This process must be encouraged. Pius describes this community as "a family of states," "family of nations," and "world community."[43]

In the community of nations, "every individual state is embedded in the international legal order and therefore in the order of natural law."[44] Like Leo XIII before him, Pius is against the right of the *fait accompli*. For this reason, he calls for "victory over the disastrous principle that usefulness is the basic reason and measure for law, that violence creates the law." It is necessary "to return to a serious and deep morality with reference to the principles of the community of nations."[45] Pius differentiates between the requirements of international law, which prescribes natural law, and positive international law. As belonging to the former, he sees "the right to exist, the right to respect and a good name, the right to individuality and one's own culture, the right of development, the

---

Romano, 24 December 1949, 2.

41. Pius XII, Nuntius Radiophonicus 24.12.1944, 18.

42. Pius XII, Iis qui interfuerunt Conventui quinto nationali Italico Unionis Iureconsultorum catholicorum, in: AAS XLV, 1953, 795 (Italian original).

43. Pius XII, Nuntius Radiophonicus 24.12.1943, in: AAS XXXXVI, 1944, 24 (Italian original).

44. Pius XII, Iis qui interfuerunt Conventui quinto nationali Italico Unionis Iureconsultorum catholicorum, 796.

45. Pius XII, Sermo . . . in pervigilio nativitatis, 24.12.1940, in: AAS XXXIII, 1941, 13 (Italian original).

right of observance of contracts between states and similar rights."[46] In contrast to this, "positive international law has to determine the requirements of nature more exactly and to adapt itself to the concrete conditions, and apart from this, it has to make regulations which correspond to the purpose of the community. Although these regulations are drawn up voluntarily, they are, just the same, binding." "Even if the content of these agreements belongs only to positive law, the duty to fulfill them emanates from nature and natural law."[47] According to this understanding of international law, every "state is directly subject to the order of international law" and can exercise its sovereignty only "within the framework of international law."[48]

3.3. An Effective International Authority

Pius XII welcomed Dumbarton Oaks's plans for the foundation of the organization of the United Nations in his 1944 Christmas message. However, he warned that the new union of nations must avoid "the structural mistakes and the failures of previous solutions" and refers here to the "absolutely valid order of being and purpose . . . which also includes the unification of humankind and the family of nations."[49] Pius can be interpreted as

---

46. The following quotations are from Pius XII, Iis qui interfuerunt Conventui quinto nationali Italico Unionis Iureconsultorum catholicorum, 795.

47. Pius XII, Allocutiones dirigentibus ac Sociis Sodalitatis Italicae, 771.

48. Pius XII, Iis qui interfuerunt Conventui quinto nationali Italico Unionis Iureconsultorum catholicorum, 796.

49. The following quotations are from Pius XII, Nuntius Radiophonicus 24.12.1944, 17-19.

meaning that the nascent United Nations needed a basis in international law, in which justice and freedom apply as absolutely necessary basic values and their validity can and must be enforced.

The main concern of a new union of nations, Pius states in his 1944 Christmas message, must be "to do everything possible to proscribe the war of aggression as a permissible solution to international tensions and as a tool of national ambitions for all time." Therefore, Pius calls for an effective international political authority with the power to enforce this. The "authority of a union of nations such as this [must] be a true and effective one . . . as regards the member states, but so that every one of them maintains the same right to its relative sovereignty." In 1944, the pope hoped that, from Dumbarton Oaks's known plans, "a body would be created, which would have, according to a common decision, the highest possible authority, and which would have the task of nipping every single threat of individual or collective attack in the bud." This explains Pius' disappointment in 1948 when the West failed to react to the Communist putsch in Czechoslovakia, a reaction he calls "unfeeling neutrality." This "indifference to the war of aggression,"[50] as he refers to the appeasement policy of 1938, had already led to immense damage in the past; that is, had been one of the causes of the World War. Therefore, the "organization of the 'United Nations' . . . must remove from its basic constitution every trace of its origins, which had necessarily been of war solidarity." Pius was here alluding to the veto right of the five powers in the Security Council with which the former Allies could block every action of the UN Security Council. His demand is still relevant today.

War can only be successfully overcome if every "law-

---

50. The following quotations are from Pius XII, Nuntius Radiophonicus 24.12.1948, 11f.

breaker is banned as a disturber of the peace to ignominious isolation outside the civilized world." Just how wide the gulf between theory and practice was became clear to the Pope in 1956 after the Hungarian uprising was smashed and the UN peace commissioners were forced to leave. "Nobody expects or demands the impossible, not even from the United Nations. But one should have been able to expect that it would have been able to exert its authority, at least by having observers in those places where essential human values were in most danger."[51] Because he "would like to see the authority of the UN increased," Pius goes far beyond the political reality of his day and repeats the demand that the UN "should have the right and the power to prevent any military intervention, under whatever pretext, by any country, and that it should take over the protection of law and order in the threatened state with a sufficiently large police force." "Recognition of the immorality" of war, therefore, is not sufficient to ban it. "The threat of legal intervention by the nations and punishment of the attacker, meted out by the community of nations"[52] is required before this ban can be effectively enforced.

Pius is cautious about the institutional organization of the United Nations. He limits himself to the basic statement that the United Nations should be formed by the agreement of the nations and be democratically and federally structured. The democratization should ensure that "according to God's order, humankind with his work within the family and society" is the object of interna-

---

51. The following quotations are from Pius XII, Nuntius Radiophonicus 23.12.1956, AAS XXXXIX, 1957, 20f (Italian original).

52. The following quotations are from Pius XII, Nuntius Radiophonicus 24.12.1944, 19.

tional order.⁵³ Hence, international authority is effective, but not absolute. It must "be a true and effective [authority] . . . for the member states, but so that each of them maintains the right to its relative sovereignty."⁵⁴ The federal structure reflects the fact that "the political world organization must correspond to the totality of the natural relationships, to the normal and organic order which regulate the relationships of humankind and the various individual nations."⁵⁵ Therefore it should keep and promote the individual way of life of a healthy human community, a society whose members work together for the good of the whole of humankind."

Let us summarize: Pope Pius XII developed an international order based on natural law. Taking God as the origin of natural law, he declared that, through recognition of the order which is in its own nature and in the nature of things, humankind finds ethical standards for the construction of a political system. Thus far, Pius was taking a traditional stance. According to Alfred Verdroß, Pius XII based his concept of an international order on the classical international law doctrine of men such as Vitoria and Suarez and "laid the foundations for its further development."⁵⁶ On these foundations, John XXIII and the Second Vatican Council (1963-65) built their concept. With his call for an effective interna-

---

53. Pius XII, Sermo... in pervigilio nativitatis, 24.12.1945, in: AAS XXXVIII, 1946, 23 (Italian original).

54. Pius XII, Nuntius Radiophonicus 24.12.1944, 18.

55. The following quotations are from Pius XII, Ad participatantes Conventui internationali de "Mouvement universel pour une Confédération mondiale," in AAS XXXXIII, 1953, 278-280 (French original).

56. Alfred Verdroß, "Erneuerung und Entfaltung der klassischen Völkerrechtslehre durch Pius XII," in: H. Schambeck, ed., Pius XII. zum Gedächtnis, 626.

tional authority which has the power to enforce the law, Pius continued where Benedict XV left off. Under this plan, the state has relative sovereignty. Pius assigned the competencies between state and international authority according to the principle of subsidiarity. Pius' stand for democracy, stemming from his experience of the Fascist and Communist dictatorship, is remarkable as democracy corresponds best to the dignity and freedom of humankind. The most important idea for him is the promotion of the democratization of the international order.

4. John XXIII: The Development of the Individual Requires Universal Common Good

John XXIII was elected Pope on 28 October 1958 after the nineteen-year pontificate of Pius XII. While Pius had been affected by the East-West conflict and religious persecution for the previous ten years, John XXIII was able to perceive the first cautious signs of détente. During both the Berlin crisis (1958-62) and the Cuban crisis (1962), Khrushchev had provoked the West, but had finally seen reason and backed down.[57] Religious persecution in the USSR decreased; pressure was taken off the church in Czechoslovakia, Poland and Hungary. John saw it as the task of his pontificate to look for ways to establish dialogue and balance beyond the blocs and thus to lay the foundations for peace. This explains the descriptive style of his encyclicals, which emphasized what was common to both sides and left out what separated Christians and Marxists.

---

57. Cf. E. Nagel and H. Oberhem, Dem Frieden verpflichtet. Konzeptionen und Entwicklungen der katholischen Friedensethik nach dem Zweiten Weltkrieg (Munich and Mainz, 1982), 35.

In his peace encyclical "Pacem in Terris" of 11 April 1963,[58] Pope John XIII started methodically with the natural law tradition,[59] just as his predecessor Pius XII had. Political peace is based on the order of natural law and can be recognized by man there: "Peace on Earth... can be firmly established only if the order laid down by God be dutifully observed." (*PT*, 1.) The laws which regulate human coexistence "are to be sought . . . in the nature of man, where the Father of all things wrote them" (*PT*, 6). According to John, human relationships on all levels of interpersonal and political life can be regulated by natural law: "By these laws men are most admirably taught, first of how they should conduct their mutual dealings; then how the relationships between the citizens and the public authorities of each State should be regulated; then how States should deal with one another; and finally how, on the other hand the community of all peoples, should act towards each other . . ." (*PT*, 7). The concept of the common good is at the center of this social doctrine: "Since men are social by nature, they are meant to live with others and to work for one another's welfare" (*PT*, 31). The common good, according to John, is furthered if every single human community, including the community of nations, bases itself on the values of truth, justice, love and freedom.[60]

---

58. John XXIII, Pacem in terris: Peace on Earth, Encyclical Letter of His Holiness Pope John XXIII, ed. William J. Gibbons (New York, 1963; hereafter cited as PT).

59. Cf. Nagel and Oberhem, Dem Frieden verpflichtet, 39.

60. Cf. PT, 35f, PT, 80.

4.1. The Universal Common Good

When John XXIII speaks of the international community, two models would be feasible. On the one hand, he might see the international community as a community of states; then it would be analogous to the national community: the state consists of individuals who join together for mutual help and protection. The members of the international community would be the states. They would then have to be the legal subjects of international law. However, it is not the individual state that Pope John sees as a constitutive member of the international community, it is the individual human being. The unity of the international community has its roots in the community inclination of human nature. "The unity of the human family," writes John, "has always existed, because its members were human beings all equal by virtue of their natural dignity." (*PT*, 132). John does not, however, give reasons from the theology of creation for this unity, as Pius had done; instead he sees it as a phenomenon of the present: "Recent progress of science and technology has . . . influenced men to work together and live as one family . . . . Relations have become closer between individuals, families and intermediate associations belonging to different political communities, and between the public authorities of those communities . . . the interdependence of national economies has grown deeper, ..., so that they become, . . ., integral parts of the one world economy" (*PT*, 130). This mutual dependence leads to a situation in which no individual state "is able to pursue its own interests and develop itself in isolation" (*PT*, 131). They need each other. "Hence," concludes John, "there will always exist the need to promote . . . the universal common good, that is, the common good of the entire human family" (*PT*, 132). From the description of the growing interdependency of humankind, John XXIII reaches the conclusion that there is a "necessity, founded in the nature of humankind, to achieve the universal common good."[61]

One could imagine that Pope John's reasoning would lead him to call for a universal political authority. If the national common good needs to be promoted by political power, then the international common good needs a universal political authority. But here too, John argues from the perspective of the individual human being. It is the task of the common good to make possible and develop individual dignity and freedom. Because the dignity of human persons is founded in the moral order, John can also morally justify both the common good and national power: "The moral order, which needs public authority in order to promote the common good in civil society, requires also that the authority be effective in attaining that end" (*PT*, 136). However, John has just explained that the interdependency of states has grown enormously and that the lifes of nations are intertwined in many areas. Individual states can no longer regulate those things which directly or indirectly affect the life of each and every person. "It can be said . . . that . . . the present system of organization and the way its principle of authority operates on a world basis no longer correspond to the objective requirements of the universal common good" (*PT*, 135). For the sake of the dignity and development of human beings, the international common good too must be promoted beyond the national common good. The rights of the

---

61. Cf. Ioannes XXIII. Pacem in terris, in: AAS LV, 1963, 292: "Hac de causa flagitabit semper necessitas, ex ipsa hominibus natura orta, ut convenienter bono universali studeatur, quod scilicet cunctae hominum familiae interest." Gibbons translated this as follows: "Hence there will always exist the objective need to promote, in sufficient measure, the universal common good, that is, the common good of the entire human family." (PT, 132.)

individual are the point of orientation for the international common good.[62] John comes to the further conclusion that this can only be secured by way of a suitable worldwide political power: "Today the universal common good poses problems of worldwide dimensions, which cannot be adequately tackled or solved except by the efforts of public authorities endowed with a wideness of powers, structure and means of the same proportions: that is, of public authorities which are in a position to operate in an effective manner on a worldwide basis. The moral order itself, therefore, demands that such a form of public authority be established." (*PT*, 137.) Like his predecessor Pius before him, John starts from the premise that the worldwide problems which need to be solved can only be solved by a worldwide public authority. John characterizes this worldwide political power, or "general political power" as he also calls it, as being founded in the common accord of all nations (*principle of consensus*) (*PT*, 138); it extends across the whole world (*principle of universality*) (*PT*, 137).

4.2. The Principle of Subsidiarity

Pope John is aware of the risk that a universal superstate could be a conclusion of this line of thinking. He therefore points to the *principle of subsidiarity*: "Just as within each political community the relation between individuals, families, intermediate associations and public authority of each political community and the public authority are governed by the principle of subsidiarity, so too the relations between the public authority of each political

---

62. Cf. PT, 139: "Like the common good of the individual political communities, so too the universal common good cannot be determined except by having regard to the human person."

community and the public authority of the world community must be regulated by the light of the same principle." (*PT*, 140.) The idea of subsidiarity, a basic principle of Catholic social ethics, is that needs have to be dealt with at the lowest practical level of the human community; only if this level cannot meet the need effectively does the next higher level of community become responsible. The classical definition of the principle of subsidiarity is in Pope Pius XI's encyclical letter *Quadragesimo Anno* of 1931: "None the less, just as it is wrong to withdraw from the individual and commit to a group what private enterprise and industry can accomplish, so it is an injustice, a grave evil and a disturbance of right order to itself functions which can be performed efficiently by smaller and lower societies."[63]

The principle of subsidiarity is supposed, on the one hand, to guide the building of a human society in such a way that freedom and personal responsibility can be realized, since the goal of each society is to enable the individuals within it to flourish. On the other hand, since no individual can flourish alone, the support of society becomes necessary at that point where the individual requires the help of others. This principle is meant to determine all relations between individual and society as well as among political communities at different levels. John XXIII therefore stresses that the "public authority of the world community is not intended to limit the sphere of action of the public authority of the individual community, much less take its place" (*PT*, 141). The political authority of the world community, as the pope understands it, "must tackle and solve problems of an economic, social, political or cultural character which are posed by the universal common good" (*PT*, 140). We have gotten used to the fact that a number of

---

63. Pius XI, Quadragesimo Anno 79, in: The Social Year Book 25 (Oxford 1934), 31.

problems can only be solved by humankind as a whole, by the international community and not by individual states: environmental questions, world hunger, peace, disarmament and a number of other issues. "For the vastness, complexity and urgency of those problems, the public authorities of the individual states are not in a position to tackle them with any hope of resolving." (*PT*, 140.) The order of priority mandated by the principle of subsidiarity can be phrased as Arno Anzenbacher does: As much competence for the lower level as possible, but only as much competence for the higher level as necessary. The principle, as can be seen, is not a recipe but a guideline. Its concrete application depends on the empirical circumstances.[64]

As a guideline to design political communities, the principle of subsidiarity has found wide acceptance. Within the European discussion of how to distribute political powers between Brussels and national capitals, the principle of subsidiarity is the accepted standard. On one hand subsidiarity is supposed to specify necessary common task of the European Union; on the other hand it helps to restrict the trend towards centralization and to strengthen the sub-state regional level, as the discussions of federalism in England and France show. An analogous debate is yet to come on the international level regarding the future development of the United Nations, if we would follow the path that John XXIII has pointed out.

5. Conclusion

This analysis has shown how the popes since Leo XIII have searched for ethical foundations of peace between the nations.

---

64. Cf. Arno Anzenbacher, Christliche Sozialethik (Paderborn, 1997), 214.

They all see a solution in abrogating the right of states to wage war without juridical limitation. Since Benedict XV, the idea has grown of an international authority, on which nations agree and which enforces the ban on war effectively. This basic concept is founded - particularly where Pius XII is concerned - in an international order based on natural law. Central to this argument are the dignity and freedom of the human being as the point of orientation of every political community. The increased interdependency of nations and the fact that the lives of people today have become so international have led to an awareness that a universal common good, beyond the national common good, is required for the further development of the human person. The necessity of an international political authority is derived from the necessity of an international common good. The international political authority should be competent, as regards individual states, and able to interfere in their sovereignty in order to promote the common good of the community of nations. If the principle of subsidiarity were to be introduced here as a guideline, the result would be a major change in the present state system. The popes do not address the problem of democratic control of the international authority in their writings.

With their demands for effective enforcement of current international law and resolute further development of international institutions, however, the popes agree with similar ideas put forward by international law experts[65] and legal philosophers.[66]

---

65. Cf. Klaus Dicke's contribution in this volume, "Sovereignty under Law", 195-215.

66. Cf. Matthias Lutz-Bachmann's contribution in this volume, "The Sovereignty Principle and Global Democracy", 217-32 and Otfried Höffe, Demokratie im Zeitalter der Globalisierung (Munich, 1999), 229ff.

Sovereignty under Law

Klaus Dicke

On the eve of the millennium session of the UN General Assembly, Secretary-General Kofi Annan addressed the question of sovereignty in a series of articles. "State sovereignty, in its most basic sense, is being redefined - not least by the forces of globalization and international co-operation," he wrote in the Economist (18 September 1999), and he added: "I fear our conceptions of national interest have failed to follow suit. A new, broader definition of national interests is needed in the new century, which would induce states to find greater unity in the pursuit of common goals and values. In the context of many of the challenges facing humanity today, the collective interest is the national interest." At the same time, a Canadian initiative at the UN to study the legality and implications of "humanitarian intervention" met serious oppisition although Canada offered to pay for it. "That wasn't considered to be prudent, because there was so much opposition to it by certain countries, as well as within the bureaucracy," Foreign Minister Lloyd Axworthy said (New York Times, September 14, 2000). Obviously, the redefinition of sovereignty, which indeed is one of the most significant results of the transitional period of international relations following the end of the Cold War, goes along with policies of sovereignty protectionism.

The following chapter will balance the processes and reasons leading to a redefinition of sovereignty against the tendencies of states to follow a policy of sovereignty protectionism. The first section will put some questions about the concept of sovereignty arising from "rethinking the state" under the conditions of globalization. Section 2 will elaborate on the changes and redefinitions that sovereignty, taken as a legal concept, went through in the progress of international law during the twentieth century and will introduce the category of "sovereignty under law." In turn, section 3 will address different political concepts of sovereignty in contemporary world politics. The concluding section will evaluate contributions by political and legal theory to redefine sovereignty from the viewpoint of whether there is a future for state sovereignty.

1. Question Marks for State Sovereignty

After the end of the Cold War, "rethinking the state" has become a common effort of international law, political science, and legal as well as political-theory scholars.[1] In the overall perspective of this question, the concept of sovereignty, which proved to be one of the most steady and solid cornerstones of the international world and of world order since the Thirty Years War, is questioned in a threefold manner: "Rethinking the state" puts a question-mark behind the concept of sovereignty because modern theories of globalization and regionalization teach us that states in general are eroding and waning in substance, that new actors are arising, and that in general the future of our world is a denationalized one beyond the nation-state and its sovereignty (cf. Delbrück 1993; Dicke 2000). On the other hand, there are voices

---

1. For a comprehensive effort to rethink the state under the conditions of globalization from the point of view of international law and the general theory of the state ("Allgemeine Staatslehre"), see Hobe 1998; Reinicke 1998, pp. 52 *et seq.*

calling to "bring the state back in" (Evans et al. 1985). They hold that in the last analysis the state remains and has to remain the main actor in and the true sovereign of international politics.

Far from being useful in resolving this ambiguity in views of sovereignty, "Catholic thought," the second element reflected in the present book, adds new question marks. On the one hand, Catholic thought in its natural-law tradition understands the state as societas perfecta and thus justifies and underlines its status as "sovereign." On the other hand, Catholic thought, again based upon its natural law tradition, upholds the notion of human rights. By doing so it gives emphasis to an idea which since the late eighteenth century counters the societas perfecta in its function of legitimizing supreme state power. So the question arises as to whether the natural law tradition upholds and enhances state sovereignty, or puts sovereignty under the condition of respect for and protection of the rights of the human person.

The third element reflected in the present book, "contemporary political theory," complicates the field even further. In the twentieth century, we have a lot of learned articles and books on, as well as definitions of, sovereignty.[2] At the same time, however, we have a lot of confusion as far as the level of analysis, the theoretical status of the notion of sovereignty, and its significance for an appropriate understanding of world order are concerned.

A closer look into debates on sovereignty in the century just ended reveals two overall tendencies and thus adds new question marks. A first tendency is represented by complaints about the triumph of state sovereignty after the First and again after the Second World War: The League of Nations Covenant as

---

2. Schreuer 1993; Chayes and Chayes 1995; Krasner 1995-96; Krasner 1999; Hobe 1998; Jackson 1999.

well as the Charter of the United Nations were criticized for paying more than due regard to the old-fashioned and peace-destroying concept of sovereignty, to the "skeleton in the closet," as Karl Loewenstein put it (1945). On the other hand, predictions of the decline or even the end of sovereignty were firmly established elements of political thought throughout the century (e.g., Albrow 1996). In those views, sovereignty is compromised by the decline of state power, by increasing duties to cooperate under international regimes (cf. Wolfrum 1992), by increasing international finance flows beyond any control by states, and by NGOs and other relevant non-state actors becoming influential in international relations. And third, to complete our confusion, we are told that nothing changed with regard to sovereignty. A first version of this thesis holds that sovereignty since 1648 has not changed inasmuch as the state functioned and continues to function as the legally independent and politically authoritative subject of international relations - I call this the realist version. A second version adds that sovereignty from the time of Bodin on had ever been understood as a normatively conditioned concept or had always been compromised by political practice. In this moderate view – I call it the functional one - sovereignty is conceptualized as authority legibus solutus in so far as it means supreme authority of legislation (whether legitimized by the substance of the state as societas perfecta or by the will of the people and the objective of securing and promoting human rights); but at the same time it is regarded as conditioned and bound by natural law itself or by more or less institutionalized balances of power both domestically and within the international system.

Instead of going into the details of any of the positions mentioned above, I would like to argue in this paper that, with regard to sovereignty, the twentieth century indeed has brought about significant and fundamental changes: changes in the scope, nature and realm of state sovereignty. I will demonstrate this in the following part of my paper by going through the most fundamental changes of international law and international practice in particular in the second half of the century.

Before going into the details of international legal developments during the twentieth century, however, some methodological preliminaries are called for. I take sovereignty, first of all, as "a legal concept whose basis in social reality requires continuous monitoring" (Meessen 1995, 1200). The term sovereignty is descriptive and prescriptive at the same time. It describes the legal and/or political position of states within the international system in general terms. As a descriptive notion, sovereignty has been defined as "the power or authority which comprises the attributes of an ultimate arbitral agent - whether a person or a body of persons - entitled to make decisions and settle disputes within a political hierarchy with some degree of finality. To be able to take such decisions implies independence from external powers and ultimate authority or dominance over internal groups" (King 1991, 492). On the other hand, sovereignty is prescriptive in so far as Article 2, paragraph 1 of the UN Charter states that "[t]he organization is based on the principle of the sovereign equality of all its Members." Under this proviso, states acknowledge state sovereignty and mutual respect for it. As a legal concept, sovereignty comprises an element of integrity but, in order to be effective, "must be protected by rules of international law of some specification delimiting the sovereign rights of one state from another" (Meessen 1995, 1194).

One of the main reasons for the confusion mentioned above is that in legal and political theory the descriptive elements of sovereignty are taken as normative ones. In order to avoid such confusion, the present paper will take sovereignty as a notion of legal and political practice or, in other words, as a category of history that gives expression to certain practical experiences, changing from time to time. In dealing with these notions of practice, as I call them, I follow the path of Kant's critical philosophy. Kant strongly opposed the methodology of ahistorical natural-law metaphysics in defining concepts metaphysically along the lines of a pre-given natural or historic order and then deriving practical consequences from such metaphysical definitions. Instead, he suggests analyzing notions of practice by critically testing them against the experience of freedom in history which, in his terminology, is called autonomy.

In this perspective, sovereignty has to be taken as the expression of autonomy by political entities, which serves to denote in shorthand their freedom from fear of civil war and from foreign domination. At the same time it stakes out their claim to recognition as equals and to autonomous subjection under agreed rules of social conduct. In this view, the concept of sovereignty meets the practical purpose of those states striving for sovereignty in the twentieth century as, for example, indicated by the "Declaration on the Granting of Independence to Colonial Countries and Peoples" (GA Res. 1514 [XV] of 14 December 1960) and by the 1970 "Declaration on Principles of International Law Concerning Friendly Relations and Co-operation among States in Accordance with the Charter of the United Nations" (GA Res. 2625 of 24 October 1970), which spells out in detail the rights and duties of states under the principle of sovereign equality of states.

2. Twentieth-Century Changes in Sovereignty under International Law

In a comment on the Dumbarton Oaks draft of the UN Charter, Karl Loewenstein wrote: "The serpent of international sovereignty, under the protective coloration of the term 'peace-loving,' has found a new abode in the shade of the Oaks of Dumbarton" (1945, 315). As correct as Loewenstein might have been in his prognosis of international behavior under Cold War conditions, he nevertheless failed to acknowledge that, especially when compared with the League of Nations Covenant, the UN Charter had changed the abode and legal context of sovereignty significantly. It introduced new elements that indeed redefined sovereignty.[3]

Whereas the League Covenant was concluded by the "High Contracting Parties," the Charter introduces the republican language of popular sovereignty: "We, the peoples of the United Nations . . . . " Without over-stressing this preamble language,[4] one can conclude that states united under the Charter regard themselves as representatives of their peoples and, consequently, can be judged by their own pretension.

A second redefinition of sovereignty results from the Charter's endeavor to establish or at least to rely on the duty of states to

---

3. With the Dumbarton Oaks proposals in mind, Pope Pius XII in his 1944 Christmas message used the notion of "relative sovereignty" (Justenhoven 2001). This notion seems adequate to meet both the UN Charter's intentions and the legal developments between 1945 and 1990.

4. For an interpretation of the Charter preamble, see Hobe et al. 1997 with further references.

cooperate. Article 1, paragraph 1 establishes that it is the purpose of the UN "to take effective collective measures for the prevention and removal of threats to the peace, and for the suppression of acts of aggression or other breaches of the peace, and to bring about by peaceful means . . . adjustment or settlement of international disputes . . . ." This proviso rests on the assumption that effective peace-keeping measures, as well as adjusting or settling disputes, in a world of sovereign equals require cooperation by states. It stipulates, in other words, implied obligations of states under the Charter.[5] If one left aside these obligations, Chapters VI and VII which spell them out could not function as elements of a public international order. Additionally, Article 1, paragraph 3, which is spelled out by Articles 55 and 56, stipulates that the UN aims "to achieve international cooperation in solving international problems of an economic, social, cultural, or humanitarian character, and in promoting and encouraging respect for human rights . . . ." Again, this proviso cannot be understood without acknowledging a bona fide duty of states to cooperate towards these ends.

Another group of legally innovative elements are the norms of the UN Charter establishing the power of the organization to deal politically with human-rights questions and at the same time establishing the right of every human being to be protected against discrimination on grounds of race, sex, language or religion (Arts. 1 para. 3; 55 c).[6] An innovative element of its own is the power of the Security Council to act on behalf of the member states (Art. 24) in carrying out its powers under Chapter VII. This important change in the legal environment of state sovereignty is underlined

---

5. For a similar reasoning on Kant's dictum "Der Friedenszustand unter Menschen . . . muß . . . gestiftet werden," see Hackel 2000, pp. 49, 69.
6. See Dicke 1995, pp. 99 et seq. with further references.

by Article 2, paragraph 7, which establishes that the principle of non-intervention "shall not prejudice the application of enforcement measures under Chapter VII." A further new element can be added: Article 103 established the priority of Charter law in case of conflict with any other international agreement. By this proviso the Charter introduced an element of "higher law" into international law. As I have argued in an earlier paper, this proviso can be understood as a significant sign of the process of constitutionalizing international law, which starts with the Charter (Dicke 1993, 1994; Fassbender 2000; Frowein 2000).

These observations can be summarized as follows: The Charter establishes sovereignty as a legal concept in the framework of an international constitution that, although based on the sovereign equality of states, breaks with the tradition of the Westphalian system of deriving all authority of international law from the sovereign will of states. As a legal concept, sovereignty changed from an exclusive authority above international law to sovereign equality under it.

This new legal framework of the UN Charter induced remarkable developments in international law and international practice after the UN had come into being (Delbrück 1995; 1996, 318–348; 1998). In this vast array, I would like to emphasize only four developments. In the field of human rights, even under Cold War conditions we witnessed a steady increase in both treaty and customary law that firmly established legal rights of human beings against states as well as standards for states' treatment of their citizens. Comparable developments of progressive constitutionalization took place in the fields of environmental protection, arms control, and the use of global commons.

As to international law of the environment, Martina Haedrich concludes that "das Souveränitätsprinzip in dem Maße modifiziert wird, als es die internationale Pflicht zur Kooperation in sich aufnimmt und damit einzelstaatlicher Souveränitätsverzicht im Interesse gemeinsamer Souveränitätsausübung erfolgt" (Haedrich 2000, 547). In international law of treaties and in international legal doctrine, too, new concepts arose that by no means can be derived from a legal order based upon state sovereignty pure and simple. Instead, they pay due regard to the redefinition of sovereignty already elaborated. First, the 1968 Vienna Convention on the Law of Treaties established the category of ius cogens. Second, the ICJ in 1970 coined the notion of international legal norms erga omnes.[7] Both categories contradict an understanding of international law as derived from state sovereignty and further promote and foster the understanding of sovereignty under law as redefined by the UN Charter and by state practice under its umbrella. Finally, the most recent practice of the Security Council under Chapter VII allows for the conclusion that the Council regards gross violations of international constitutional law - of fundamental human rights, of the integrity of the global environment, or of the non-proliferation of nuclear arms - as "threat[s] to the peace" under Article 39 of the Charter.[8]

And following up on its anti-apartheid policy, the UN General Assembly as well as other international organs overcame their Cold War-induced reluctance to judge the domestic constitutional order of states. Among others, the Baltic states experienced international pressure to apply international standards in their minority legislation. The UN, the EU, the Council of Europe, OSCE and other organizations are engaged in assisting and monitoring democratization processes. And the government of Austria

---

7. For both concepts, see Delbrück 1993; Dicke 1993; Delbrück 1996; each with further references.
8. Further evidence is given by Dicke 1997.

recently got a new sense of European solidarity when European governments put political ethics as enshrined in the constitutional law of the European Union and in international law above their acceptance of a government coalition containing a party whose commitment to those ethics was in doubt.

To summarize this section, then: Starting with the UN Charter, international law fundamentally changed the legal status, validity and environment of sovereignty, effectively redefining it. The notion of sovereignty under law seems adequate to describe this new legal status of sovereignty. Hegel's view that international law was defined by sovereign decisions of states was replaced by the view that, in contrast, it is sovereignty that is defined by international law. This notion of sovereignty under law, however, raises a lot of questions: Is "sovereignty under law" still sovereignty at all? What are the consequences of the developments as analyzed so far? In which direction do we have to rethink the state? It is with those questions that political theory comes in. The following section will prepare the ground for some new theoretical considerations on the sovereignty of states.

3. Political Understanding and Meaning of Sovereignty

In September 2000 the state of Tuvalu became the 189th sovereign equal in the United Nations. Tuvalu has 9,100 inhabitants, 12 among them being members of Parliament; its territory covers 26 square kilometers. What is bringing up this extreme case meant to emphasize? First of all, it demonstrates the crucial fact that in international relations we do not find sovereignty as such, but states that claim to be sovereign and that in terms of power are, to say the least, different. Second, the admission of Tuvalu is a - historically very late - expression of the common experience that in the second half of the twentieth century led to a struggle for sovereignty and recognition (for "legal sovereignty" in Krasner's terms, 1999, 14) and thus politicized the notion of sovereignty. Third, by its admission Tuvalu gained rights of membership and of participation in the organs and proceedings of, inter alia, the UN, which made it different from, for instance, Quebec or California.[9] Tuvalu became a global player; it gained "interdependence sovereignty" (again following Krasner 1999). The most important lesson to learn from Tuvalu's admission, however, seems to be that the globalization of statehood is one of the most important political developments of the twentieth century.

To understand the political meaning of sovereignty in the globalizing world of ours, however, it is important to distinguish different perceptions and positions taken by states with regard to sovereignty. Because sovereignty is a category of practice, as elaborated above, perceptions of it are conditioned by different historical experiences, different positions, and different interests. Three classes of experiences, positions, and interests can be distinguished.

For the overwhelming majority of states that gained admission to the UN after 1955, sovereignty above all meant recognition by the international community. This was true for those states which came into being as a result of decolonization, but it was also true for the GDR and other socialist countries. Most of them jealously rejected any effort by other states, groups of states, or international organizations to intervene in what they called their domestic affairs. This political coin is still valid today, and we will have to test its validity.

---

9. For similar reasoning see Taylor 1999, p. 142.

A second group of states regards sovereignty mainly as an entitlement to international participation. This is true for most members of the so-called "OECD-world," for states, in other words, that rely on a relatively long history of statehood and that in the twentieth century to a large degree entered into regional and/or international cooperation or even transferred parts of their sovereignty to supranational organizations like the EU. Their concern with sovereignty aims at minimizing their costs and their "vulnerability" (Keohane and Nye 1977, 12-19) and at improving their international bargaining position and their standing within the community of states.

A third group of states is no group at all but the only remaining superpower. It is not by chance that in US politics the sovereignty debate has very special features: Neither recognition nor vulnerability in webs of international cooperation seems to be necessarily of prior or major concern in American politics. The US does not claim, it executes sovereignty. Its unique position in world politics has two aspects: first, a virtually inexhaustible potential for international leadership, and second, a very high degree of veto power. The very existence of the UN is a result of the first; its financial malaise during the last two decades is a result of the second aspect.

These remarks lead to a distinction of some importance for any future political theory of sovereignty, namely, the distinction between internal and external sovereignty; and this distinction is closely related to the question of who is really sovereign. I will take this distinction as a starting point for my concluding considerations on the future of state sovereignty.

4. The Future of State Sovereignty - Is There Any?

The concept of sovereignty emerged from the experience of civil wars. Raggione di stato, suprema potestas, or state authority as put forth by Machiavelli, Bodin and Hobbes aimed at an institutional setting and an understanding of states that allowed and regarded them to be law- and peace-making entities.[10] Only the political theory of the nineteenth and twentieth centuries distinguished between internal and external sovereignty, and one of the most important results of the world-wide striving for external sovereignty and its recognition was the universalization of statehood as mentioned above. The main challenge to sovereignty resulting from processes of globalization, however, is that internal sovereignty or, in more political-science language, the state's steering capacity, is in jeopardy.

In this framework, Wolfgang H. Reinicke argues that the "challenges faced today by the nation-state are primarily challenges to internal, not external sovereignty," while "the nation-state as an externally sovereign actor in the international system will become an institution of the past" (1998, 230). He calls for a search for a functional equivalent to replace territoriality in order to be "better equipped to meet the specific challenges of globalization" (ibid.).

From a European perspective, it is one of the most important results of the integration process of the European Union and of the related transformation of Western democracies that European states indeed have started to replace the principle of territoriality by principles of functional competence. Trends toward corporatism, the involvement of non-state actors in finding solu-

---

10. For an in-depth study of sovereignty in the history of ideas, see Quaritsch 1986.

tions for political problems, lean state policies and other developments indicate that in European politics to a remarkable degree it is civil society itself which is in the process of taking over political functions that formerly fell within the realm of internal sovereignty. In this process, the role of the nation-state which is further diminished by increasing patterns of intergovernmental cooperation within a multi-level European system of governance boils down to the function of authoritatively laying down regulations for solving conflicts, taking decisions and distributing public resources for basic public purposes like education, social security and participation in international relations.

With regard to external sovereignty, Chayes and Chayes in 1995 topped the argument for increasing international interdependence by arguing that "for all but a few self-isolated nations, sovereignty no longer consists in the freedom of states to act independently, in their perceived self-interest, but in membership in reasonably good standing in the regimes that make up the substance of international life." And further: "To be a player, the state must submit to the pressures that international regulations impose. . . . Sovereignty, in the end, is status - the vindication of the state's existence as a member of the international system" (1995, 27). Although it is possibly an exaggeration to assume that the "new sovereignty" of status proposed by Chayes and Chayes is a first step towards an international or a global civil society in which states, international organizations and non-state actors will more or less function as sovereign equals, various international regimes indicate that the solution of global problems produces global policy clubs consisting of internationally acknowledged scientists, representatives of NGOs, officers of international organizations, and national governmental officials. Those functional clubs can be referred to as international civil society in a nutshell.

This section has argued that political theory should develop a clear picture of both the decline of internal and the change in external sovereignty, and that it should also be prepared to replace the secular notion of sovereignty by "civil society in a global public order," its demands and its connotations. But two questions remain: what will be the remaining status of sovereignty and of sovereign states in the future world of "civil society," and what can catholic thought contribute to conceive it? Even in the world of "civil society" authoritative decisions to uphold a legal order in the global public interest will be called for, and authoritative decisions can be taken by representative agents only. Even a civil society is in need of institutions, and as long as no better solutions are found it will rely on the institutions provided by the state. So in the end, sovereignty and sovereign states will survive, but their survival and acceptance depends on their ability to represent what Kant referred to as the "salus rei publicae," which in a globalizing world can only be found in a permanent dialogue with global civil society.

Catholic thought always reached out for universality. When it is the main challenge to political theory in the forthcoming future to seek solutions for the problem of finding adequate political structures, legal regulations, and policy strategies to represent humankind as a whole in framing global civil-society politics, three possible contributions of Catholic thought come to my mind. (1) The unity of humankind is not the least heritage of Catholic thought. The rich traditions of Catholic thought in interpreting the unity of humankind in terms of a theology of creation or a theology of salvation seem to be quite useful in fostering the perception of humankind as the unique subject of global politics. (2) One of the most important contributions by Catholic thought to the general theory of the state is its theory of the common good in terms of pluralism, human rights and self-government of a global civil society. Although in my view the common good when derived from natural law prescriptions along the lines of a Thomistic tradition often results in empty formulas, a well-founded theory of the common good is one of the main challenges of the future world to political theory. In this regard, the development of papal teaching on global public authority in the 20th century as analyzed by Justenhoven (2002) meets the growing experience of the international community that in a globalized world any public authority has to be tested against global public interests. The call for an effective global public authority, the search for a global common good and the principle of subsidiarity articulate related experiences and aspirations of today's humankind. (3) In interpreting these elements of papal teaching while keeping in mind modern political experiences, Catholic thought can help to get a better and deeper understanding of modern international law developments. Political settings as the League of Nations or the United Nations and legal norms as well are historic attempts to establish conditions for a secure life in freedom and dignity. The development of sovereign states and of an international law based upon the equal sovereignty of states were answers to challenges of freedom. Today, the internationalization and globalization bring up new challenges which - as the Second Vatican Council put it (cf. Justenhoven 2002) - call for "a universal public authority, recognized by all, which will possess the effective means on behalf of all to safeguard security, the observance of justice and respect for rights". Responsiveness to this call requires political experience guided by a commitment to justice and freedom or, in short, practical reason. Catholic thought has its part in promoting, recognizing and enlightening this very requirement of practical reason.

References

Albrow, Martin, The Global Age: State and Society Beyond Modernity. Cambridge, 1996.

Annan, Kofi A, "Two concepts of sovereignty," in The Economist, 18 September 1999.

Chayes, Abram, and Chayes, Antonia Handler, The New Sovereignty: Compliance with International Regulatory Agreements. Cambridge and London, 1995.

Delbrück, Jost, "Globalization of Law, Politics, and Markets," Indiana Journal of Global Legal Studies 1 (1993): 9-36.

Idem (ed.), Allocation of Law Enforcement Authority in the International System. Berlin, 1995.

Idem, Die Konstitution des Friedens als Rechtsordnung. Berlin, 1996.

Idem, "Von der Staatenordnung über die internationale institutionelle Kooperation zur 'supraterritorial or global governance': Wandel des zwischenstaatlichen Völkerrechts zur Rechtsordnung des Menschen und der Völker?", in Ulrich Bartosch, Jochen Wagner (eds.), "Weltinnenpolitik". Münster, 1998, pp. 55-71.

Dicke, Klaus, "Interventionen zur Durchsetzung internationalen Ordnungsrechts: konstitutives Element der neuen Weltordnung?," Jahrbuch für Politik 3 (1993): 259-83.

Idem, "Die UN-Charta – Ausbau und ungenutzte Möglichkeiten," in Hanns-Seidel-Stiftung (ed.), Nach Überwindung des Ost-West-Konflikts: Gedanken zur "Neuen Weltordnung." München, 1994, pp. 48–75.

Idem, "Interventionsoptionen der Staatengemeinschaft im Bereich des Menschenrechtschutzes," in Hartmut Jäckel (ed.), Ist das Prinzip der Nicht-Einmischung überholt? Baden-Baden, 1995, 95–115.

Idem, "National Interests vs. the Interests of the International Community: A Critical Review of Recent Security Council Practice," in Jost Delbrück (ed.), New Trends in International Lawmaking: International Legislation in the Public Interest. Berlin, 1997, pp. 145–69.

Idem, "Erscheinungsformen und Wirkungen von Globalisierung in Struktur und Recht des internationalen Systems auf universaler und regionaler Ebene sowie gegenläufige Renationalisierungstendenzen," in idem et al. (eds.), Völkerrecht und internationales Privatrecht in einem sich globalisierenden internationalen System: Auswirkungen der Entstaatlichung transnationaler Rechtsbeziehungen. Heidelberg, 2000, pp. 13-44 (English summary 42-44).

Evans, Peter B., Rueschemeyer, Dietrich, and Skocpol, Theda (eds.). Bringing the State Back In. Cambridge, 1985.

Fassbender, Bodo, "Souveränität," in Helmut Volger (ed.), Lexikon der Vereinten Nationen. München/Wien, 2000, pp. 492–95.

Frowein, Jochen A, "Konstitutionalisierung des Völkerrechts," in idem et al. (eds.), Völkerrecht und Internationales Privatrecht in einem sich globalisierenden internationalen System: Auswirkungen der Entstaatlichung transnationaler Rechtsbeziehungen. Heidelberg, 2000, pp. 427–47.

Hackel, Volker Marcus, Kants Friedensschrift und das Völkerrecht. Berlin, 2000.

Haedrich, Martina, "Internationaler Umweltschutz und Souveränitätsverzicht: Eine Untersuchung zum Wandel des Souveränitätsverständnisses," Der Staat 39 (2000): 547-69.

Hobe, Stephan, Der offene Verfassungsstaat zwischen Souveränität und Interdenpendenz: Eine Studie zur Wandlung des Staatsbegriffs der deutschsprachigen Staatslehre im Kontext internationaler institutioneller Kooperation. Berlin, 1998.

Jackson, Robert (ed.), Sovereignty at the Millennium. Malden and Oxford, 1999.

Justenhoven, Heinz-Gerhard, "Peace through a Public Global Authority in Papal Teaching from Leo XIII to John XXIII," in this volume, 167-94; Keohane, Robert O., and Nye, Joseph S. Power and Interdependence: World Politics in Transition. Boston and Toronto, 1977.

Keohane, Robert O, "Hobbes' Dilemma and Institutional Change in World Politics: Sovereignty in International Society," in Hans-Henrik Holm and Georg Sorensen (eds.), Whose World Order? Uneven Globalization and the End of the Cold War. Boulder, San Francisco, and Oxford, 1995, pp. 165-86.

King, Preston, "Sovereignty," in David Miller (ed.), The Blackwell Encyclopedia of Political Thought. Cambridge and Oxford, 1991, pp. 492–95.

Krasner, Stephen D, "Compromising Westphalia," International Security 20 (1995-96): 115-51.

Idem, Sovereignty: Organized Hypocrisy. Princeton, 1999.

Loewenstein, Karl, "The Serpent in Dumbarton Oaks," Current History 8 (1945): 310-16.

Meessen, Karl M., "Sovereignty," in Rüdiger Wolfrum (ed.), United Nations: Law, Policies and Practice. München/Dordrecht, 1995, 2: 1193-1201.

Quaritsch, Helmut, Souveränität: Entstehung und Entwicklung des Begriffs in Frankreich und Deutschland vom 13. Jahrhundert bis 1806. Berlin, 1986.

Reinicke, Wolfgang H, Global Public Policy: Governing without Government? Washington, D.C., 1998.

Schreuer, Christoph, "The Waning of the Sovereign State: Towards a New Paradigm for International Law?" European Journal of International Law 4 (1993): 447-71.

Taylor, Paul, "The United Nations in the 1990s: Proactive Cosmopolitanism and the Issue of Sovereignty," in Robert Jackson (ed.), Sovereignty at the Millenium, Malden and Oxford, 1999, pp. 116–43.

Wolfrum, Rüdiger, "International Law of Cooperation," in Rudolf Bernhardt (ed.), Encyclopedia of Public International Law, 1995, 2: 1242–47.

The Sovereignty Principle and Global Democracy: Thoughts on Transforming the System of States, Based on Kant

Matthias Lutz-Bachmann

As the twentieth century drew to a close, political philosophy underwent a remarkable renaissance. Influenced not least by the debates on John Rawls' *Theory of Justice*[1], its attention had until then been focused on the problem of a normative grounding for the system of laws, and an interpretation of the constitution of the democratic state as a legitimate, because just, legal system. Yet as the ongoing renaissance of political philosophy continues to unfold, the pressure of economic-cum-technological rationalisation processes, potentiated by the end of the East-West conflict, is at the same time changing not only the social contexts of policymaking, but also the very system of state action. Chiefly those changes described under the categories of increasing globalization of economic agency, transnationalization of legal systems, and the emergence of a global public, raise the issue of whether or not the key concepts and premises of traditional political philosophy still apply, and whether or not they are still appropriate to describe

---

Translated by John Cochrane

1. See John Rawls, A Theory of Justice (Cambridge, Mass., 1971).

present political reality. These concepts include the notion of an undivided and indivisible sovereignty of the state, a politico-legal assumption that had been the dominant concept in policymaking and political theory from Jean Bodin[2] up until the Charter of the United Nations.[3] Indeed, it remains a fixed article of dogma in traditional national and international law. Perhaps it is due to the close relationship between the discourse of contemporary political philosophy, and a jurisprudence that proceeds by generating formal, in some cases normative arguments, that political philosophy to date has only just begun elaborating the categories needed to conceptualize the lasting change that the system of nation state agency has undergone in the face of the most recent modernisation and globalization processes.

These developments towards a global society have brought lasting change to the object of political philosophy. Yet they are not the sole causes of the radical, structural loss of sovereignty by the traditional nation state that is unfolding before our very eyes. Relatively independently of the processes of economic globalization, in recent decades the older assumption of a largely unlimited sovereignty of the state has become questionable, in the first instance with respect to the society within its own territorial borders. At least it would seem that a sharp conceptual and terminological distinction between the state and society, and between public and private law as having two precisely separate purviews, is less self-evident today than was supposed by traditional political philosophy when its terms were coined in the eighteenth and early nineteenth centuries. These developments are to a significant extent founded in the inherent logic of politics itself, which is to

---

2. Jean Bodin, Les six livres de la république (Paris, 1576), vol. 1.
3. See esp. Articles 1-6 of the Charter of the UN.

say in an expansion of the tasks of the state, as a result of which the expectations placed on political decision-making, the competencies of policymaking, and thus the *modus operandi* of the sovereign state all change.[4] In brief, while it was once the prime task of the liberal capitalist state bound by the rule of law to ensure the internal and external security of its citizens, it did so by instituting a state monopoly on coercion, while separating the three public powers. The state thus emerged as the sole proprietor of sovereign rights that, according to the theories of popular sovereignty, had been transferred to it by the body politic. However, whereas the liberal capitalist state attempted to guarantee by means of its constitution only the formal conditions of possibility for individual self-determination, for the reconcileation of social interests, and for the economic success of its citizens, the modern welfare state – in response to the unsolved problems of the capitalist economy – also intervenes in social and economic processes, and by putting in place a sustainable state-guaranteed system of welfare benefits helps actively foster the reproduction of economic and social vitality. Only through an active economic and social policy did the welfare state succeed in integrating all sections of the population into the democratic polity, and thus also in guaranteeing realization of the ideas of popular sovereignty. In the recent past and the present, a growth in irrefutable tasks of the state, and spheres of political action, has been observed. Despite all the contrary assertions of a rollback of the state in certain areas, this is leading not only to an ongoing expansion of state competencies to embrace new spheres of action, but also to a qualitative change in state action, which is having a lasting impact on the relationship between the state and society. For instance, these developments

---

4. See, e. g., Dieter Grimm, Staatsaufgaben (Frankfurt/M, 1996).

mean that the state is facing an increasing number of tasks to shape the future of society and the economy, such as framework planning, the development and financing of new cost-intensive technologies, the assessment and minimization of risks associated with those new technologies, the prevention of threats to internal and external security, as well as threats to the health of the population – not only within its own borders – and not least threats to future generations and the natural environment. This list of tasks through which the state is required to intervene preventively and help steer ongoing processes demonstrates that the majority of these decision on highly complex issues often cannot be revoked at all in the short term, or can be revoked only with great difficulty, by shifts in the democratic majority within the electorate.[5]

As the number of such decisions affecting the future life of society as a whole continues to increase, this entails a change in the contexts of political action that is having a sustained impact on the sovereignty of state action. It is with good reason that sociological analyses of these changes are speaking of losses of the sovereignty of the state in its societal context. I would like to emphasise three aspects of this process in which the sovereignty of the state, both within its own borders, and beyond them (that is, in both the national and international contexts), has changed in Europe and certainly not only there:

First: Within the state (or at the national level) we observe that the agencies of state coercion are able to discharge their tasks less and less through sovereign legislative decision-making and direct executive intervention, and more and more through new, often seemingly corporatist forms of cooperation with social groups. This can, as Dieter Grimm, a former member of the

---

5. See, e. g., Ulrich Beck, Risikogesellschaft (Frankfurt/M, 1996).

German constitutional court, has pointed out, lead as far as a partial depletion of jurisdiction because, as he observes, "Where there is no intervention, there is no provision of legality, where there is no provision of legality, there is no law binding upon the administration, where there is no law binding upon the administration, there is no monitoring of lawfulness by the courts."[6] This is tending to lead to a relinquishment of state sovereignty in many spheres within the polity, to a neo-corporatist cooperation between the agencies of state coercion with social groups, private enterprise or associations, and overall to an increase in the status of private law relative to public law. It is beyond question that this is at the same time leading to a loss of transparency and in some cases a loss of scope for sovereign democratic decision-making. Unlike Niklas Luhmann[7] or Helmut Willke[8] who have also noted these phenomena, I see this recent metamorphosis of the state not only in terms of system theory as a rollback of the sovereign functions of the state vis-à-vis individuals or other sub-systems of society, which would in part be entirely welcome, but also to some extent as a problematic delegitimation of the political sphere and a loss of democratic agency. The stakeholders in this process are primarily individual citizens, whose status as agents and "original" subjects of inalienable rights is in any case considered largely irrelevant by the sociological theories based on Luhmann.

---

6. Grimm, p. 636.
7. See Niklas Luhmann, Das Recht der Gesellschaft (Frankfurt/M, 1995), pp. 407-495.
8. See Helmut Willke, Die Entzauberung des Staates: Überlegungen zu einer sozietalen Steuerungstheorie (Königstein, 1983), pp. 1117-149, or H. Willke, Supervision des Staates (Frankfurt, 1997).

Second: To the extent that the tasks of averting external threats, securing the future, preventing risks, guaranteeing frameworks conducive to successful economic action, ensuring sustainable economic development, and guaranteeing welfare systems can no longer be performed sustainably and effectively by a single state, states are transferring implementation of these tasks to supra-national associations, organizations, or actors, which in fact means that a part of the sovereignty of nation states is being transferred to those institutions. What in the political practice of the period immediately after the Second World War began as the partial transfer of sovereignty to security alliances in order to avert the external threat of war, a development initially unproblematic in terms of democratic theory, has, as a result of the internal changes within societies and economies, gathered a momentum of its own. This is leading to the proliferation of new transnational actors and supra-national administrative procedures, and thus to the introduction of a largely independent sphere of international law, whose authorship is becoming increasingly ill-defined, whose application is becoming increasingly difficult to monitor, and whose judgment in courts of law is increasingly falling within the purview of an international jurisdiction. This development is creating a situation in which states are increasingly transferring away core sovereign rights, without the new international actors and organizations themselves being accorded the quality of sovereign institutions, and without them being directly democratically accountable to the sovereign, the international community (of nation states), or the individuals immediately affected (the stakeholders) themselves.

Third: Only now, against this background of a gradual self-dissolution of the classical principle of state sovereignty, caused by transformation within societies and the development of their economies, are the tendencies towards the emergence of a global society beginning to unfold their impacts on the relationships between nation states. Although the end of the East-West conflict may have been politically conducive to this ongoing process, it was certainly not its source. The margins of the society for which today's state must perform its sovereign function of creating and maintaining legal and policy frameworks are becoming less and less congruent with the territorially-defined borders of the individual states lastingly affected by these developments. The rapid coalescence of global financial markets and the global expansion of trade and communication systems, which are increasingly undermining all the state's mechanisms of steering and control, the rising mobility of populations, goods, and individuals, and the permeability of borders are not only creating increased risks for both politico-economic systems and individuals. They are also creating a growing number of tasks that individual nation states are ultimately no longer able to solve on their own. The internationalization of almost all segments of the political sphere is a manifest expression of these developments.[9] The globalization process is at the same time leading to "closer global social relations,"[10] as a result of which events that are initially of only regional import can suddenly take on global significance. Via this route, even actors whose radius of action is locally defined are increasingly able to interact with other agents on a global, direct and immediate basis. In other words they are able to influence the actions of other actors without the mediacy of the traditional nation states and their governments or parliaments.

In this situation of dramatically changed contexts of state and political action, a number of critical objections have been

---

9. See David Held, Democracy of the Global Order (Cambridge, 1995).

10. See Anthony Giddens, Konsequenzen der Moderne (Frankfurt/M., 1997), p. 85.

raised, and a number of proposals made. Some of them I would like to mention in this presentation, and others not. The latter include arguments put forward ostensibly in the interests of "cultural identity"[11] or in the name of welfare statehood, advocating a strengthening or restitution of the traditional notion of the sovereignty, that is, that of a territorially defined nation state more or less autonomous in its actions by virtue of its constitution. In defence of the aforementioned tendencies, a policy of "cultural identity" or protection of traditional social welfare standards is advocated, which certainly amounts to a closure of borders to the outside world and a more or less moderate protectionism. A discussion of such proposals would need to demonstrate in detail that a definition of the state as a historically organic cultural nation, or as a welfare nation constituted by the membership dues paid by its insured citizens, at the same time involves a policy that, in view of the changed tasks and contexts, will place the individual state in the uncomfortable position of being more likely in the long run to fail to achieve than to actually achieve the goals of state which its protagonists have set it, namely to maintain the aforementioned cultural and/or welfare nation. However, in the face of a global society undergoing radical upheaval, calls for protectionism of whatever political hue will certainly not be helpful in addressing the political problems that arise, since the structural prerequisites that would have been the condition of possibility for practical realization of protectionist hopes have already largely disintegrated. Presumably, an isolated return by individual states to economic policy strategies à la John Maynard Keynes will not be especially successful, for the same reason.

---

11. See, e. g., Charles Taylor's contribution to that debate in Multiculturalism and the "Politics of Recognition" (Princeton, 1992).

I will have to leave out any more detailed discussion of this theme, however, because it seems to me to be more important in this situation to discuss another, more normative problem of political philosophy. That problem consists of the fact that the growing loss of sovereignty by the individual state also goes hand-in-hand with a de facto political and structural loss of legal power by the hitherto democratic sovereign, namely the state nations, or more specifically their respective electorates. Discussion of this issue proves difficult, since it is not easily possible to dispute either the democratic legitimacy of the described processes themselves, or their appropriateness; they did not simply happen to or impose themselves on the democratic sovereigns concerned without repeated, albeit perhaps all too sporadic declarations of intent. Furthermore, no one will deny the right in principle of non-governmental actors such as individuals or organizations acting peacefully to act in the global arena. Finally, there can be no denying the expediency of authorising supranational institutions to act in an executive or jurisdictional capacity in certain problem areas, such as global issues of environmental protection, power production, or peacekeeping, and perhaps even in monitoring global respect for human rights. Nevertheless, the cumulative outcome of these developments would appear to be an inevitable delegitimation of democratically constituted political agency. Therefore, the question that political philosophy must answer is this: How can the process of transferring sovereign rights from the level of the territorially defined nation state "inwards" to society, "downwards" into the regions, and "outwards" to transnational and supra-statal institutions be steered so that, as developments continue to unfold, we do not encounter a problematic dissolution of the normatively well-founded link between the sovereignty principle and democracy?

In response to the problem raised I would like to draw on an argument drawn from basic assumptions of Kant's philosophy of law.[12] This argument contains a provisional conceptual apparatus for addressing the issue of how the normative idea of a democratic state bound by the rule of law, legitimated by the electorate, can be reconciled with the political challenges thrown up by a globalized economy. As readers are aware, Kant seeks to elaborate a theory of the legitimate polity based on the idea of legal relations to be demanded a priori. His argument is also based on the inevitable interaction of individual agents, also termed legal persons ("Rechtspersonen"). In his philosophy of law, Kant presents us with his reasons for rejecting the idea of a public law extending beyond the boundaries of sovereign states, compelling him in other words to reject the idea of the so-called "world republic." Yet his arguments are not convincing, for a number of reasons. For one thing, in rejecting the idea Kant gets caught up in contradictions. Second, Kant argues from premises that to some extent no longer apply today in the way that Kant was able to presuppose for his own time. I would include among those premises both the aforementioned principle of territoriality of the modern state and the axiom of sovereignty, which traditional political philosophy was able to take as read. At the same time, the dissolution of the significance of national borders in addressing the challenges faced by the state today, and the dissolution of the sovereignty of state agency, both within and beyond a state's territorial borders,

---

12. The general question of how to apply Kant's political philosophy to problems of the international politics of today, is discussed in James Bohman and Matthias Lutz-Bachmann, Perpetual Peace: Essays on Kant's Cosmopolitan Ideal (Cambridge, Mass., 1997) or in Hauke Brunkhorst, Wolfgang Köhler, and Matthias Lutz-Bachmann, Recht auf Menschenrechte (Frankfurt/M, 1999).

formerly held to be absolute, the complementary processes of globalization and regionalization now also threaten the democratic principle of the modern state, articulated since the eighteenth century as the principle of popular sovereignty.

For the purposes of my argument I would like to draw on the two principles that Kant introduces in the jurisprudential section of his *Metaphysics of Morals*, to demonstrate the reasonable imperative of the transition from the so-called "natural condition" (status naturalis) to the "civil condition" (status civilis). These are the principle of the "exeundum ex statu naturali" and the "law of permission." The first principle is taken as formulating the notion that a state must be left behind in which people encounter one another with conflicting legal claims that cannot be peacefully reconciled through application of public law shared both by the agents concerned and by others, because jointly constituted by them. The second principle, on the other hand, formulates the idea of permission under certain circumstances to also compel another person to leave the natural legal condition and accede to the purview of a common (because in principle jointly constituted) public law. From the validity of these two principles Kant infers the rationally grounded legitimacy and necessity of a democratic constitutional state, characterized by the inherent principle of the separation of powers and grounded in the principle of popular sovereignty.

In the area of political acting that is more and more determined by the processes of globalization and regionalization, we encounter a situation that displays similarities to the "natural legal condition" outlined by Kant and that, according to him, every man and woman is required to leave, "unless he or she wants to renounce any concepts of right." In this situation, each person must reach agreement "with all others (with whom he or she cannot avoid interacting)" that all must submit to public lawful external coercion, and "so must leave the state of nature" and "enter into a condition in which what is to be recognized as belonging to them is determined by law and is allotted to them by adequate power (not their own but an external power); that is, they ought above all else to enter a civil condition."[13] For the state bound by the rule of law that Kant advocates, however, a further requirement is that its legislative power shall be the sole prerogative of the "united will" of the people, which Kant further defines as the "concurring and united will of all," and qualifies with the statement "insofar as each decides the same thing for all and all for each, and so only the general united will of the people, can be legislative."[14]

The changed space of political agency caused by globalization corresponds precisely to the "natural legal condition" outlined by Kant, in that people and not, as traditional international law has assumed, states or their representatives, meet directly or indirectly and interact in a fashion relevant to the law. Yet when doing so they do not comply with principles of justice or legal provisions that proceed from their "united will." Where they do not act entirely within the sphere of private law, which they supplement and thus further develop through contracts and agreements, their actions are subject to different systems of public law, and certainly not the sphere of a public law postulated by Kant proceeding from their joint democratic consensus-building process. Yet precisely this fact places the present situation in a light that, from a Kantian perspective, leaves the legal system looking deficient. The fact that the global private law and the system of global governance, driven by a few national governments, establishing themselves in the

---

13. Immanuel Kant, The Metaphysics of Morals, § 44, trans. Mary Gregor (Cambridge, 1996), p. 90.
14. Ibid., § 46, p. 91.

course of globalization, are no longer due to any "common will" or democratic sovereign is in the light of a Kantian prospective a lamentable state of affairs, exacerbated by the fact that states are exposed to an ongoing erosion of their sovereign rights of action both within and beyond their territorial borders. This development is not the outcome of bad policymaking, however, but the result of a change in the structures of political acting that now allows states only this option for political action to address the tasks created by the complex processes of globalization and regionalization. In this situation it is necessary to draw from Kant's idea of founding a democratic state, formulated under the economic, political and social conditions of more or less "closed societies" in the eighteenth century, the positive notion that a system of public law of transnational or global application is needed, including new forms of a global legislation and a worldwide criminal jurisdiction in cases of severe crimes against human rights. This new global public legal sphere must go beyond the present system of international law, because and inasmuch as the authors of international law are states and their organs charged with the mandate of representing the ostensibly sovereign state beyond its borders. The authors or subjects of the "global law" I am advocating would – according to Kant's arguments – need to be those legal persons (natural persons and juridical personalities) who, as a result of globalization, interact in a manner directly relevant to the law, who could then only assert their private or particular interests without employing or threatening to employ physical or institutional coercion or other forms of power, lawfully, if the law they follow proceeds from the "consensual and united will of all."

A globally applicable world law proceeding from the "united will" of the world's citizens would have to take into account the fact that, unlike the case of transition from the natural legal condition to the republican state advocated by Kant, the present situation already includes spheres of democratically legitimated law, that is, states bound by the rule of law, which would then also need to be embraced by global law. The constitution of a global law would therefore have to be confined to those functions that, for the reasons already mentioned, are not yet or no longer performed by traditional national or international law. This complex division of tasks within a public law with differential normative claims concerning its reach and competence would be congruent with the described changes in the space of state agency to which the principles of territoriality and sovereignty are exposed. In line with the principle of shared sovereignty emerging here, global law should not form the underpinnings of a "global state" based on the eighteenth-century model and centralizing all power and legal competence. It is rather the case that structures of a public law going beyond traditional national and international law are becoming established globally and forming the legal framework for global political action by nation states, associations of states, and continental states, as well as for global action by regional institutions and non-governmental actors. The framework competence of a global law also at the same time implies a limited competence, although that would have to include the fundamental task of guaranteeing certain minimum standards worldwide, such as protection of the most elementary legal goods. Consequently, the prime task of a global law would be to secure worldwide the basic rights formulated as human rights and establish effective procedures of legal protection, as are currently being discussed by the United Nations in the context of establishing a permanent international criminal jurisdiction.[15] I would also include among the tasks

---

15. See, e. g., Leila Nadya Sadat and S. Richard Carden, "The New International Criminal Court: An Uneasy Revolution," Georgetown Law

of global law, and its organs legitimated through the consent of the world's population, *first* of all and most especially peacemaking, that is, the administrative institutionalization of a prohibition on war, which would need to be preceded by an internationally binding disarmament policy. *Second*, the guarantee of every person's right to life, liberty, and security of person, the right to recognition as a person before the law, and the right of all the world's citizens to equal treatment before the law without discrimination and equal protection in the event of any of these rights being infringed, and the right to effective remedy. *Third*, the right to freedom of thought, conscience, and religion, the legal guarantee of which will have consequences for the political frameworks governing education and the media. *Fourth*, the creation of frameworks for protection of the natural environment and protection of the human genome, and *fifth*, legal measures to guarantee a minimum provision to people of goods vitally important to their physical survival, which, in accordance with the principle of distributive justice, would include a minimum standard of food, water, and health-care provision.

This function of a global public law geared to protecting and enforcing basic human rights thus calls for a certain degree of global statehood reaching beyond the traditional territorial boundaries of the nation state. This form of global statehood has the advantage of eliminating those ambivalences that had hitherto emerged in the debate on human rights as either moral rights or basic republican rights. At the same time, the form of global statehood here proposed also proves necessary from a legal point of view, assuming that we do not wish to leave the process of globally networked action entirely to private actors in the capitalist sector and their mighty advocates, in other words if the idea of democracy – now understood globally – is not to be abandoned and the "old European" principle of the political autonomy of individuals is not to be consigned to the past. This response to the challenges of globalization that I am proposing from the perspective of legal philosophy, in other words this form of global statehood, should not be understood as a "mega-state" with all the attributes of the previous states of European modernity. It should rather be viewed as a form of graduated sovereignty within a wider body politic, enabling actors to draw distinctions between a range of levels of competence and policymaking and to organize them along horizontal and vertical lines. This form of global statehood would need to be determined by the equally rationally imperative principles of subsidiarity and federalism. The task of these principles would first be to ensure that competence for addressing a given political issue would rest primarily in the hands of those immediately affected by it, and second to put legal and political frameworks in place to foster the integration of all politically relevant levels such as local government, regional government, federal states, nation states, and continental states, thus averting any possibility of emergent hegemonies or dissociation.

Authors

Norbert Brieskorn SJ, Professor of Philosophy of Law and Social Philosophy, Hochschule für Philosophie (Jesuit College of Philosophy), Munich

Klaus Dicke, Professor of Political Theory and History of Ideas, Friedrich-Schiller-Universität, Jena

Penny Gill, Mary Lyon Professor of Humanities and Professor of Politics, Mount Holyoke College, Massachusetts

Heinz-Gerhard Justenhoven, Dr. theol., Director of Institut für Theologie und Frieden (www.ithf.de), Barsbüttel/ Hamburg

Stephen D. Krasner, Graham H. Stuart Professor of International Relations, Stanford University, California

Matthias Lutz-Bachmann, Professor of Philosophy, Johann Wolfgang Goethe-Universität, Frankfurt/Main

James Bernard Murphy, Associate Professor of Government, Dartmouth College, Hanover, New Hampshire

Kenneth Pennington, Kelly-Quinn Professor of Ecclesiastical and Legal History, The Catholic University of America, Washington, D. C.

James Turner, Cavanaugh Professor of Humanities *and, until 2003,* Director of the Erasmus Institute (www.nd.edu/~erasmus), University of Notre Dame, Indiana

Wissenschaftliche Paperbacks
Politikwissenschaft

Hartmut Elsenhans
Das Internationale System zwischen Zivilgesellschaft und Rente
Gegen derzeitige Theorieangebote für die Erklärung der Ursachen und die Auswirkungen wachsender transnationaler und internationaler Verflechtung setzt das hier vorliegende Konzept eine stark durch politökonomische Überlegungen integrierte Perspektive, die auf politologischen, soziologischen, ökonomischen und philosophischen Ansatzpunkten aufbaut. Mit diesem Konzept soll gezeigt werden, daß der durch Produktionsauslagerungen/Direktinvestitionen/neue Muster der internationalen Arbeitsteilung gekennzeichnete (im weiteren als Transnationalisierung von Wirtschaftsbeziehungen bezeichnete) kapitalistische Impuls zur Integration der bisher nicht in die Weltwirtschaft voll integrierten Peripherie weiterhin zu schwach ist, als daß dort nichtmarktwirtschaftliche Formen der Aneignung von Überschuß entscheidend zurückgedrängt werden können. Das sich herausbildende internationale System ist deshalb durch miteinander verschränkte Strukturen von Markt- und Nichtmarktökonomie gekennzeichnet, die nur unter bestimmten Voraussetzungen synergetische Effekte in Richtung einer autonomen und zivilisierten Weltzivilgesellschaft entfalten werden. Dabei treten neue Strukturen von Nichtmarktökonomie auf transnationaler Ebene auf, während der Wiederaufstieg von Renten die zivilgesellschaftlichen Grundlagen funktionierender oder potentiell zu Funktionsfähigkeit zu bringender, dann kapitalistischer Systeme auf internationaler und lokaler Ebene eher behindert.
Bd. 6, 2001, 140 S., 12,90 €, br., ISBN 3-8258-4837-x

Klaus Schubert
Innovation und Ordnung
In einer evolutionär voranschreitenden Welt sind statische Politikmodelle und -theorien problematisch. Deshalb lohnt es sich, die wichtigste Quelle für die Entstehung der policy-analysis, den Pragmatismus, als dynamische, demokratieendogene politisch-philosophische Strömung zu rekonstruieren. Dies geschieht im ersten Teil der Studie. Der zweite Teil trägt zum Verständnis des daraus folgenden politikwissenschaftlichen Ansatzes bei. Darüber hinaus wird durch eine konstruktivspekulative Argumentation versucht, die z. Z. wenig innovative Theorie- und Methodendiskussion in der Politikwissenschaft anzuregen.
Bd. 7, 2003, 224 S., 25,90 €, br., ISBN 3-8258-6091-4

Politik: Forschung und Wissenschaft

Klaus Segbers; Kerstin Imbusch (eds.)
The Globalization of Eastern Europe
Teaching International Relations Without Borders
Globalization and fragmentation, weakly controlled flows of information and knowledge, increasing cleavages in societies undergoing rapid change, flows of migrants, services and capital, bypassing the control of national governments, life styles and consumption patterns produced by electronic media and advertising – all these developments already have a significant impact on post-Soviet regions. And all kind of actors – decision makers, journalists, experts, students – perceive the environment beyond their respective national borders increasingly as the "playground" they have to take into account, and as a framework for action.
The chapters in this volume are produced by experts in the so called transformation countries in Eastern Europe. They address various questions on inter- and transnational relations, thereby offering a framework for reflection and for analysis of macro-trends around policy fields relevant for the countries in Central and Eastern Europe. The product certainly mirrows the specific environment of researchers, teachers and students in these countries. At the same time, it reflects a process of intensive discussion on the state of IR literature worldwide. Furthermore, this book demonstrates how useful teaching tools for universities and institutes not only in Eastern and Central Europe can be produced.
Bd. 1, 2000, 600 S., 35,90 €, br., ISBN 3-8258-4729-2

Hartwig Hummel; Ulrich Menzel (Hg.)
Die Ethnisierung internationaler Wirtschaftsbeziehungen und daraus resultierende Konflikte
Mit Beiträgen von Annabelle Gambe, Hartwig Hummel, Ulrich Menzel und Birgit Wehrhöfer
"Die Ethnisierung der internationalen Wirtschaftsbeziehungen und daraus resultierende Konflikte" lautete der Titel eines Forschungsprojekts, das diesem Band zugrunde liegt. Es geht um die Themen Handel, Migration und Investitionen. In drei Fallstudien werden die Handelsbeziehungen zwischen den USA und Japan, die Einwanderung nach Deutschland bzw. Frankreich und das auslandschinesische Unternehmertum untersucht. Die Ergebnisse des Projekts sehen Hummel und Menzel in den späteren Ereignissen bestätigt: Ethnisierende Tendenzen können sich in der Handelspolitik und der Investitionstätigkeit von Unternehmen nicht durchsetzen, während die

LIT Verlag Münster – Hamburg – Berlin – London
Grevener Str./Fresnostr. 2 48159 Münster
Tel.: 0251 – 23 50 91 – Fax: 0251 – 23 19 72
e-Mail: vertrieb@lit-verlag.de – http://www.lit-verlag.de

Ethnisierung im Bereich der Migration andauert.
Bd. 2, 2001, 272 S., 30,90 €, br., ISBN 3-8258-4836-1

Theodor Ebert
Opponieren und Regieren mit gewaltfreien Mitteln
Pazifismus – Grundsätze und Erfahrungen für das 21. Jahrhundert. Band 1
Das grundlegende und aktuelle Werk eines Konfliktforschers, der über Jahrzehnte in pazifistischen Organisationen, in sozialen Bewegungen und in Gremien der Evangelischen Kirche gearbeitet hat. Ebert breitet in anschaulichen Berichten und doch in systematischer Ordnung die Summe seiner Erfahrungen aus und entwickelt Perspektiven für eine Welt, die mit der Gewalt leben muss, doch Gefahr läuft, an ihr zugrunde zu gehen, wenn sie auf die Bedrohungen keine neuen, gewaltfreien Antworten findet.
Aus dem Vorwort: "Es gibt eine pragmatische Befürwortung des gewaltfreien Handelns in innenpolitischen Auseinandersetzungen durch eine Mehrheit der Deutschen, und dies sollten wir als tragenden Bestandteil der Zivilkultur nicht gering schätzen. Doch die Frage, wie man mit gewaltfreien Mitteln regieren und sich gegenüber gewalttätigen Extremisten durchsetzen kann und wie man sich international behaupten und Bedrohten helfen kann, ist bislang kaum erörtert worden... Dieses Buch soll klären, was unter politisch verantwortlichem und doch radikal gewaltfreiem Pazifismus zu verstehen ist, und wie mit gewaltfreien Mitteln nicht nur opponiert, sondern auch regiert werden kann."
Bd. 3, 2001, 328 S., 20,90 €, br., ISBN 3-8258-5706-9

Theodor Ebert
Der Kosovo-Krieg aus pazifistischer Sicht
Pazifismus – Grundsätze und Erfahrungen für das 21. Jahrhundert. Band 2
Mit dem Luftkrieg der NATO gegen Jugoslawien begann für die deutschen Nachkriegspazifismus ein neues Zeitalter. Ebert hat sich über Jahrzehnte als Konfliktforscher und Schriftleiter der Zeitschrift "Gewaltfreie Aktion" mit den Möglichkeiten gewaltfreier Konfliktbearbeitung befasst. Von ihm stammt der erste Entwurf für einen Zivilen Friedensdienst als Alternative zum Militär.
Aus dem Vorwort: "Wer sich einbildet, auch in Zukunft ließe sich aus großer Höhe mit Bomben politischer Gehorsam erzwingen, unterschätzt die Möglichkeiten, die fanatische Terroristen haben, in fahrlässiger Weise. Jedes Atomkraftwerk ist eine stationäre Atombombe, die von Terroristen mit geringem Aufwand in ein Tschernobyl verwandelt werden kann. Wir haben allen Grund, schleunigst über zivile Alternativen zu militärischen Einsätzen nachzudenken und die vorhandene Ansätze solch ziviler Alternativen zu entwickeln."
Bd. 4, 2001, 176 S., 12,90 €, br., ISBN 3-8258-5707-7

Wolfgang Gieler
Handbuch der Ausländer- und Zuwanderungspolitik
Von Afghanistan bis Zypern
In der Literatur zur Ausländer- und Zuwanderungspolitik fehlt ein Handbuch, dass einen schnellen und kompakten Überblick dieses Politikbereichs ermöglicht. Das vorliegende Handbuch bemüht sich diese wissenschaftliche Lücke zu schließen. Thematisiert werden die Ausländer- und Zuwanderungspolitik weltweiter Staaten von Afghanistan bis Zypern. Zentrale Fragestellung dabei ist der Umgang mit Fremden, das heißt mit Nicht-Inländern im jeweiligen Staat. Hierbei werden insbesondere politische, soziale, rechtliche, wirtschaftliche und kulturelle Aspekte mitberücksichtigt. Um eine Kompatibilität der Beiträge herzustellen beinhaltet jeder Beitrag darüber hinaus eine Zusammenstellung der historischen Grunddaten und eine Tabelle zur jeweiligen Anzahl der im Staat lebenden Ausländer. Die vorgelegte Publikation versteht sich als ein grundlegendes Nachschlagewerk. Neben dem universitären Bereich richtet es sich besonders an die gesellschaftspolitisch interessierte Öffentlichkeit und den auf sozialwissenschaftlichen Kenntnissen angewiesenen Personen in Politik, Verwaltung, Medien, Bildungseinrichtungen und Migranten-Organisationen.
Bd. 6, 2003, 768 S., 98,90 €, gb., ISBN 3-8258-6444-8

Harald Barrios; Martin Beck; Andreas Boeckh; Klaus Segbers (Eds)
Resistance to Globalization
Political Struggle and Cultural Resilience in the Middle East, Russia, and Latin America
This volume is an important contribution to the empirical research on what globalization means in different world regions. "Resistance" here has a double meaning: It can signify active, intentional resistance to tendencies which are rejected on political or moral grounds by presenting alternative discourses and concepts founded in specific cultural and national traditions. It can also mean resilience with regard to globalization pressures in the sense that traditional patterns of development and politics are resistant to change. The book shows the that the local, sub-national, national, and regional patterns of politics and development coexist with globalized structures without yielding very much ground and in ways which may turn out to be a serious barrier to further globalization. Case studies presented focus on Venezuela, Brazil, the Middle East, Iran, and Russia.
Bd. 7, 2003, 184 S., 20,90 €, br., ISBN 3-8258-6749-8

LIT Verlag Münster – Hamburg – Berlin – London
Grevener Str./Fresnostr. 2 48159 Münster
Tel.: 0251 – 23 50 91 – Fax: 0251 – 23 19 72
e-Mail: vertrieb@lit-verlag.de – http://www.lit-verlag.de

Forschungsberichte Internationale Politik

im Auftrag der Arbeitsstelle Transatlantische Außen- und Sicherheitspolitik, Fachbereich Politische Wissenschaft, Freie Universität Berlin, herausgegeben von Ingo Peters

Hildegard Bedarff
Die Wirkung internationaler Institutionen auf die Energie- und Umweltpolitik
Weltbank, EU und Europäische Energiecharta in Polen und in der Tschechischen Republik
Unter welchen Bedingungen wirken internationale Institutionen auf innerstaatliche Politikprozesse ein? Diese Studie zeigt, daß internationale Institutionen besonders dann auf substaatliche Reformen einwirken können, wenn sich die Empfängerländer in einer Umbruchsituation befinden, in der die Regierung noch keine Richtungsentscheidung getroffen hat und die gesellschaftlichen Gruppen noch nicht klar konturiert sind.
Aus umweltpolitischer Perspektive wird untersucht, inwiefern die internationalen Institutionen ihren eigenen Ansprüchen gerecht werden und einen Wandel zu einer ökologisch tragfähigen Energiewirtschaft unterstützen. In der umweltpolitischen Forschung in den internationalen Beziehungen stehen bisher internationale Umweltregime im Vordergrund. Hier wird dafür plädiert, daneben auch Wirtschaftsorganisationen, die sich mit ökologisch sensiblen Bereichen, wie der Energiepolitik beschäftigen, gleichberechtigt zu untersuchen. Die umweltpolitischen Wirkungen der drei untersuchten Institutionen sind schwach, da sie ihre ökologischen Ziele bisher noch nicht mit ihrer ökonomischen Ausrichtung verbunden haben und da gleichzeitig die ökologische Modernisierungskapazität der Empfängerländer begrenzt ist.
Bd. 26, 2000, 272 S., 25,90 €, br., ISBN 3-8258-4790-x

Cornelius Friesendorf
Der internationale Drogenhandel als sicherheitspolitisches Risiko
Eine Erklärung der deutschen und US-amerikanischen Gegenstrategien
Dieser Band ist im Rahmen eines Forschungsprojektes zu internationalen Sicherheitsrisiken entstanden. Ziel des Bandes ist es, die deutschen und US-amerikanischen Strategien gegen den internationalen Drogenhandel zu erklären und Unterschiede zu erklären. US-amerikanische Politiker versuchen, das Drogenangebot durch repressive Maßnahmen zu verringern. Die Vereinigten Staaten üben diplomatischen Druck auf Drogenanbau- und Transitstaaten aus, gehen teilweise unilateral vor und setzen ihre Streitkräfte gegen den Drogenhandel ein. Deutsche Entscheidungsträger dagegen setzen Anbau- und Transitstaaten kaum unter Druck und betrachten Unilateralismus und Militäreinsätze zur Lösung des Drogenproblems skeptisch. Erklärungsfaktoren für die unterschiedlichen Strategien sind unterschiedliche Risikowahrnehmungen, politisch-militärische Kulturen und Institutionen.
Bd. 27, 2001, 208 S., 25,90 €, br., ISBN 3-8258-5326-8

Peter Barschdorff
Facilitating Transatlantic Cooperation after the Cold War
An Acquis Atlantique. Copublished with Palgrave, New York
Why are Europe and America still allied? After all, many observers predicted after the Cold War that NATO might collapse, trade disputes could escalate, and political relations would suffer in the absence of a common threat (like the one formerly posed by the former Soviet Union). Peter Barschdorff argues that an acquis atlantique is holding the two sides together. Common experiences, legal stock and understandings make decision-makers converge their views on controversial issues, such as peace-making in the Balkans, NATO reform and trade of agricultural goods. The acquis might change over time. But as an analytic concept and as a driver of transatlantic politics it will remain an important constant.
Bd. 28, 2001, 256 S., 20,90 €, br., ISBN 3-8258-5434-5

Joanna Lucia Bodenstein
Frankreichs Antwort auf das Ende des Ost-West-Konflikts
Die Reaktion des politischen Systems auf den Umbruch 1989
In Umbruchphasen der internationalen Beziehungen gewinnt die Sicherheitspolitik einen besonderen Stellenwert; sie beinhaltet Anforderungen und Gestaltungsspielräume zugleich. Der Fall der Berliner Mauer 1989 ist Symbol für das Ende des Ost-West-Konflikts und eine historische Zäsur, die Europas Sicherheitsarchitektur grundlegend veränderte.
Diese Studie analysiert Frankreichs Handlungsspielraum nach dem Mauerfall zwischen Autonomieanspruch und zunehmender internationaler Interdependenz. Welche Politik verfolgte Frankreich gegenüber der deutschen Vereinigung, wie entwickelte sich Frankreichs internationaler Rang? Welche Antworten gab die französische Politik auf die neuen Fragen an die nationale Verteidigung und die Reform der Bündnisstrukturen? Wie reagierte Frankreich auf die gesamteuropäischen Herausforderungen, u. a. die

LIT Verlag Münster – Hamburg – Berlin – London
Grevener Str./Fresnostr. 2 48159 Münster
Tel.: 0251 – 23 50 91 – Fax: 0251 – 23 19 72
e-Mail: vertrieb@lit-verlag.de – http://www.lit-verlag.de

EU-Osterweiterung?
Bd. 30, 2002, 344 S., 25,90 €, gb., ISBN 3-8258-5877-4

Fragen politischer Ordnung in einer globalisierten Welt
herausgegeben von Prof. Dr. Friedrich Kratochwil
(Universität München)

Alexander Mutschler
Eine Frage der Herrschaft
Betrachtungen zum Problem des Staatszerfalls in Afrika am Beispiel Äthiopiens und Somalias
Insbesondere in Staaten der sog. Dritten Welt kommt es immer wieder zu Fällen von Staatszerfall, die im Extremfall, wie etwa in Somalia, zum Verschwinden von staatlichen Strukturen führen. In dieser Arbeit wird Staatszerfall mit Hilfe politischer Begriffe und Faktoren analysiert. Zum einen wird nach der Funktionalität und Legitimität der Herrschaft des Staates, zum anderen nach der Rolle von in Konkurrenz zum Staat stehender Herrschaftsverbände gefragt. Vor diesem Hintergrund wird in zwei Fallstudien, Äthiopien und Somalia, die Entwicklung dieser Staaten seit Ende des zweiten Weltkriegs bis zum Niedergang der Militärdiktaturen zu Beginn der 90er Jahre betrachtet.
Bd. 1, 2002, 360 S., 25,90 €, br., ISBN 3-8258-6138-4

Doris A. Fuchs; Friedrich Kratochwil (eds.)
Transformative Change and Global Order
Reflections on Theory and Practice
The world at the beginning of the 21st century is fundamentally different from what it was only 50 years ago – or so it seems. In the political realm, scholars identify deep changes in organization. What are the new institutions and qualities of political order? Debates on this question have focused on two concepts in particular: globalization and global governance. Using these concepts as entrance points, therefore, the contributors to this volume explore theory and practice of political organization in a transformed/ing world with the aim of shaping the post-globalization discussion.
Bd. 2, 2002, 272 S., 20,90 €, br., ISBN 3-8258-6374-3

Markus Lederer
Exchange and Regulation in European Capital Markets
This book explores how the wild beast of finance can be better understood and controlled. Using the framework of exchange and regulation, European capital markets are analyzed and it is shown that a common European area of financial exchange has developed. Concerning financial regulation, one can see that the EU has become the most dominant rule setter and the regulation established can be interpreted as being of a statutory kind. Showing the shortcomings of this process, the set-up of a more transparent megaregulator to control all financial market segments and financial agents is proposed.
Bd. 3, 2003, 312 S., 24,90 €, br., ISBN 3-8258-6954-7

Philipp S. Müller
Unearthing the Politics of Globalization
During times of transformative change, politics take place on the level where we imagine the world. *Unearthing the Politics of Globalization* offers a framework, vocabulary, and procedure to describe and access these politics. The *metaphorological approach* offered in the book allows us to demarcate the politics of globalization. Together with *philosophical therapy*, a technique that allows us to therapeutically engage policy makers, these politics can actually be accessed. The policy field of communicating foreign policy is used as a miner's canary in order to assess the fruitfulness of such an approach.
Bd. 4, 2003, 200 S., 20,90 €, br., ISBN 3-8258-6955-5

Regensburger Schriften zur Auswärtigen Politik
herausgegeben von Prof. Dr. Stephan Bierling
(Universität Regensburg)

Robert Kulzer
Demokratieverständnis und demokratische Praxis des African National Congress (1994 – 1999)
Mit den ersten freien Wahlen vom April 1994 ist die Befreiungsbewegung African National Congress (ANC) zur bestimmenden Regierungspartei in Südafrika geworden. Aufgrund des überwältigenden Rückhaltes in der schwarzen Bevölkerung wird der ANC die politische Zukunft des Landes auf absehbare Zeit maßgeblich gestalten. Vom ANC hängt es ab, wie – und ob – sich die junge und ungefestigte Demokratie in Südafrika entwickeln wird.
Die Analyse der ersten fünf Regierungsjahre des ANC zeichnet nicht nur anhand konkreter Entwicklungen den Umgang des ANC mit demokratischen Institutionen nach und zeigt damit die demokratische Praxis des ANC als Partei und als Regierung auf, sondern sie erschließt aus dem Handeln, aber vor allem aus den Aussagen und Dokumenten des ANC auch dessen theoretisches Demokratieverständnis. Im Ergebnis wird deutlich, dass die zentrale Stellung des ANC sehr

L<small>IT</small> Verlag Münster – Hamburg – Berlin – London
Grevener Str./Fresnostr. 2 48159 Münster
Tel.: 0251 – 23 50 91 – Fax: 0251 – 23 19 72
e-Mail: vertrieb@lit-verlag.de – http://www.lit-verlag.de

wohl ein Risiko für die Entwicklung der Demokratie in Südafrika darstellt.
Bd. 1, 2001, 192 S., 25,90 €, br., ISBN 3-8258-5131-1

Hans-Joachim Bauer
Der Europarat nach der Zeitenwende 1989–1999
Zur Rolle Straßburgs im gesamteuropäischen Integrationsprozeß
Bei seiner Gründung im Jahr 1949 stand der Europarat im Zentrum der europäischen Zusammenarbeit und Integration. In den darauffolgenden Jahrzehnten liefen ihm jedoch andere Organisationen den Rang ab. Ein Schattendasein war die Folge. Erst mit dem Zusammenbruch des Ostblocks und dem Ende der Spaltung Europas Ende der achziger und in den neunziger Jahren rückte Straßburg wiederum verstärkt in den Blickpunkt der europäischen Politik. Die Studie untersucht, welche Rolle der Europarat in den Jahren zwischen 1989 und 1999 spielte und ob er den – nicht zuletzt von seiten der mittel- und osteuropäischen Reformstaaten in ihn gesetzten – hochgesteckten Erwartungen gerecht werden konnte. Im Mittelpunkt der Analyse steht dabei die Osterweiterung der Straßburger Organisation, die zu einer problematischen Aufweichung ihrer für den Kontinent so wichtigen Prinzipien geführt hat. Außerdem wird das Verhältnis Straßburgs zu EU und OSZE beleuchtet, das von sektoraler Doppelarbeit und mangelnder Abstimmung geprägt ist.
Bd. 2, 2001, 368 S., 25,90 €, br., ISBN 3-8258-5178-8

Dorothea Lamatsch
Euro versus Dollar
Die währungspolitische Integration Europas aus US-amerikanischer Perspektive 1969–1999
"Wake up, America!" – mit dieser Aufforderung versuchten Wissenschaftler die Aufmerksamkeit der Amerikaner auf die währungspolitischen Aktivitäten der Europäischen Union zu lenken. Die Einführung des Euro im Jahr 1999 markierte den vorläufigen Höhepunkt einer 30-jährigen Entwicklung in Europa. Aber auch die Handelspartner, allen voran die USA, sind von den Folgen dieses Schritts betroffen. Manche Auguren sagten sogar das Ende der Dollar-Hegemonie voraus. Das vorliegende Buch analysiert, wie die US-Administrationen seit 1969 – begleitet von stürmischen internationalen Währungsbeziehungen – die Entwicklung hin zur Einheitswährung verfolgt haben.
Bd. 3, 2002, 240 S., 17,90 €, br., ISBN 3-8258-5946-0

Texte zu Politik und Zeitgeschichte
herausgegeben von Hans Karl Rupp
(Universität Marburg)

Wolfgang Hecker; Joachim Klein; Hans Karl Rupp (Hg.)
Politik und Wissenschaft. 50 Jahre Politikwissenschaft in Marburg
Band 1: Zur Geschichte des Instituts
Die Marburger Politikwissenschaft ist bekannt – ihre Geschichte weniger. Der erste Band dieser Festschrift zum 50-jährigen Jubiläum zeichnet die Entwicklung des Fachs und der Institution nach: Von der Berufung Wolfgang Abendroths 1951, den Jürgen Habermas treffend als "Partisanenprofessor im Lande der Mitläufer" charakterisierte, über die Phase der Revolte und Hochschulreform (End-60er und 70er Jahre) bis hin zur "Professionalisierung" ab den 80er Jahren.
Ganz im Unterschied zu gängigen (Vor-)Urteilen ist die Geschichte der Marburger Politikwissenschaft vielschichtig, von Kontroversen, aber auch von hohem wissenschaftlichen Output geprägt. Und sie ist spannend zu lesen. Kenntnisreich und kompetent dargestellt von ehemaligen und derzeit Lehrenden.
Im Mai 2001 wird ein Symposium kritische Bilanz ziehen und Perspektiven für die Marburger Politikwissenschaft diskutieren.
Bd. 1, 2001, 408 S., 24,90 €, br., ISBN 3-8258-5440-x

Wolfgang Hecker; Joachim Klein; Hans Karl Rupp (Hg.)
Politik und Wissenschaft. 50 Jahre Politikwissenschaft in Marburg
Band 2
Bilanz der Marburger Politikwissenschaft – zu diesem Thema fand anläßlich des 50-jährigen Bestehens des Instituts ein Symposium statt, dessen wichtigste Ergebnisse in diesem zweiten Band der Festschrift dokumentiert werden. Perspektiven der Marburger Politikwissenschaft – im Verständnis von Politikwissenschaft als moderner Demokratiewissenschaft entwickeln alte und junge, langjährige und neuberufene Lehrende zukunftsfähige Schwerpunkte für Forschung und Lehre im Hauptteil dieses Bandes. Was ist aus den Absolventenjahrgängen 1993 bis 2000 geworden? Die Ergebnisse der 2. Marburger Absolventenbefragung runden das Buch ab.
Bd. 2, 2003, 448 S., 24,90 €, br., ISBN 3-8258-5441-8

A. Kai-Uwe Lange
George Frost Kennan und der Kalte Krieg
Eine Analyse der Kennanschen Variante der Containment Policy
Bd. 3, 2001, 368 S., 30,90 €, gb., ISBN 3-8258-5436-1

LIT Verlag Münster – Hamburg – Berlin – London
Grevener Str./Fresnostr. 2 48159 Münster
Tel.: 0251 – 23 50 91 – Fax: 0251 – 23 19 72
e-Mail: vertrieb@lit-verlag.de – http://www.lit-verlag.de

Julia Isabel Geyer
Rechtsextremismus von Jugendlichen in Brandenburg
Brandenburg befindet sich seit einigen Jahren in den Statistiken rechtsextremer Gesetzesverletzungen unter den ersten Plätzen. Zwar sind auch in Westdeutschland rechtsextremistische Einstellungen weit verbreitet. Dennoch tritt insbesondere die rechte Gewalt Jugendlicher in Ostdeutschland manifester in die öffentliche Wahrnehmung. Nur beide Faktoren zusammen, Verhalten und Einstellungen, können Aufschluss geben über die Verbreitung von Rechtsextremismus.
Den Fragen, ob der Rechtsextremismus in Brandenburg und in Ostdeutschland insgesamt ein spezifisches Jugendproblem ist, welche Strukturen er annimmt, wie weit er verbreitet ist und woraus er resultiert, wird in diesem Buch nachgegangen. Die Analyse verschiedener Brandenburger Maßnahmen und Initiativen gegen rechts zeigt hingegen trotz allem, dass es verfehlt wäre, verallgemeinernd vom „braunen Osten" zu sprechen.
Bd. 4, 2002, 168 S., 15,90 €, br., ISBN 3-8258-6004-3

Geschichte der internationalen Beziehungen nach 1945
herausgegeben von Prof. Dr. Ingeborg Koza und Dr. Thomas Stahl

Ingeborg Koza
Deutsch-sowjetische Kontakte in Politik, Wirtschaft, Wissenschaft und Kultur 1963–1967
Eine Untersuchung zu den auswärtigen Beziehungen der Bundesrepublik Deutschland
Unter Berücksichtigung der weltpolitischen Interdependenz erfolgt in diesem Buch eine Darstellung der schon in den 1960er Jahren unterhalb der Regierungsebene trotz aller ideologischen Gegensätze realisierten vielfältigen Begegnungen zwischen Menschen aus der Bundesrepublik Deutschland und der Sowjetunion. Zu den Besuchern des jeweils andern Landes zählten Kommunalpolitiker, Wissenschaftler, Experten, z. B. für U-Bahnbau, Energieversorgung, Wohnungsbau, Gesundheitswesen, Wasserwirtschaft, Postwesen, außerdem Journalisten, Schriftsteller, Frauenvertreterinnen und junge Leute. Ihre manchmal sehr subjektiven Berichte geben Aufschluss nicht nur über das Erlebte, sondern auch über die Denkweise und die politische Geprägtheit des jeweiligen Schreibers.
Bd. 2, 2002, 168 S., 17,90 €, br., ISBN 3-8258-6212-7

George C. Marshall European Center for Security Studies

Jürgen Kuhlmann; Jean Callaghan (Editors)
Military and Society in 21st Century Europe
A Comparative Analysis
After the Cold War came to an end, European countries in both East and West faced the common question of how their military organizations and those of their neighbors would respond to shifts in international relations affecting their economies, their perception of globalized threats, and cross-national security management. It is undisputed, for example, that in well-developed democratic societies, the challenge to the legitimacy of the military in society, the decreasing subjective apprehension of threat, and growing opposition to systems of universal conscription have been linked to gains in wealth and living standards. This volume seeks, by empirically measuring social indicators, to assess the current state of civil-military relations in a number of countries in Eastern Europe (Bulgaria, Czech Republic, Hungary, Romania, Russia) as well as the state of relations in several of their Western European counterparts (France, Germany, Italy, the Netherlands). The country studies describe and analyze the differing positions of the military in their specific national settings.
Bd. 1, 2000, 384 S., 35,90 €, br., ISBN 3-8258-4449-8

Jürgen Rose; Johannes Ch. Traut (Editors)
Federalism and Decentralization
Perspectives for the Transformation Process in Eastern and Central Europe
The Marshall Center research project on "Federalism and Decentralization in Eastern and Central Europe" was designed to cooperatively explore ways to promote the decentralization of formerly centralized political structures in Central and East European States, and to present models of federalism that could help introduce or strengthen federal structures in these countries. It was developed by the research department of the Marshall Center in cooperation with two reputable institutes, the European Center for Research on Federalism at the University of Tübingen and the German Institute for Research on Federalism at the University of Hannover.
Bd. 2, 2001, 384 S., 45,90 €, gb., ISBN 3-8258-5156-7

LIT Verlag Münster – Hamburg – Berlin – London
Grevener Str./Fresnostr. 2 48159 Münster
Tel.: 0251 – 23 50 91 – Fax: 0251 – 23 19 72
e-Mail: vertrieb@lit-verlag.de – http://www.lit-verlag.de